VORWORT

Crossing Over baut auf dem Niveau eines mittleren Schulabschlusses auf. In zehn Schritten (*Steps*) werden die Fähigkeiten (*Skills*) erläutert und geübt, die Grundlagen des Textverständnisses und der Textproduktion bilden (siehe Inhaltsverzeichnis oben). In jedem *Step* wird eine *Skill* in Einzelschritten erklärt, die dazugehörigen Aufgaben werden durch Kommentare in deutscher Sprache begleitet. Zu jedem *Step* gehört ein ausführlicher *Practice*-Teil mit vertiefenden Übungen, die auch die prüfungsrelevanten Aufgabenformen beinhalten. Die gängigsten Themen des ersten Semesters werden durch interessante, authentische Texte, Bilder, Cartoons und Statistiken eingeführt und dargestellt. Das Lernniveau steigt vom ersten bis zum zehnten *Step* kontinuierlich an.

Crossing Over ist für das Selbststudium wie für den Klassenunterricht geeignet; das gesonderte Lösungsheft bietet Schülerinnen und Schülern die Möglichkeit, ihre Arbeit selbst zu kontrollieren.

Alle Texte, die Sie in den nächsten drei Jahren lesen, werden viele neue, unbekannte Wörter enthalten. Was tun?

Aufgeben? Kommt nicht in Frage! Im Wörterbuch blättern? Dauert zu lang! Es ist viel zu mühsam, jedes Wort nachzuschlagen. Hirn einschalten? Ja! Es gibt einfache Strategien, wie man sich einem Text annähern kann. Die genauere Arbeit folgt erst danach.

Legen wir los!

Starting to read

Es gibt zwei bewährte Techniken, wie man sich einem Text schnell annähern kann.

- **Den Inhalt vorhersehen (*predicting*):** Schauen Sie sich zuerst folgende Bestandteile an, um Hinweise über den Text zu bekommen.
  - Die Aufgaben: In Inhaltsfragen verstecken sich oft etliche Hinweise zum Text.
  - Titel, Untertitel und Bilder: Sie sind dazu da, Ihr Interesse am Text zu wecken, und verdeutlichen daher den Inhalt.
  - Der erste und letzte Satz oder Absatz: Oft wird hier die Kernaussage des Textes gemacht.
- **Den Inhalt überfliegen (*reading for gist*):** Bei dieser Lesetechnik liest man über Unklarheiten zunächst einfach hinweg, um die Kernaussage eines Textes zu erfassen.
  - Lassen Sie sich von unbekannten Wörtern nicht aufhalten: Oft werden sie aus dem Zusammenhang klar, oder es kommt etwas später im Text eine sinngemäße Entsprechung. (→ STEP 2)
  - Konzentrieren Sie sich auf die Schlüsselwörter: Es sind meistens Substantive und Verben, die für das Verständnis wichtig sind, manchmal auch die dazugehörenden Adjektive/Adverbien.

Diese Techniken können auch später für Sie nützlich sein, z. B. wenn sie schnell herausfinden wollen, ob ein Text oder ein Zeitungsbericht lesenswert ist.

Lesen Sie diese Fragen zum Text auf der Seite gegenüber, ohne bereits den Zeitungsbericht zu kennen. Sie können die Fragen natürlich noch nicht beantworten, aber Sie bekommen einen ersten Eindruck, worum es geht. Aufgabe 1 fasst grob zusammen, wovon der Zeitungstext handelt.

Questions on the text

1 Where was the woman working?
2 What was wrong with the man?
3 What did the woman do to help him?
4 How did she know what to do?
5 What did the paramedic say about the woman's actions?
6 What does the woman think about hospital programmes on TV?

Aufgabe 1

Use the words from the box below to complete a rough summary of what might be in the text. The first missing word has been added for you.

somebody • somehow • something • somewhere

A woman was working *somewhere* [1] when ____________ [2] happened to a man. The woman did ____________ [3] to help the man. ____________ [4] she knew what to do. ____________ [5] said ____________ [6] about what the woman had done. The woman thinks ____________ [7] about hospital programmes on TV.

____ /6 Punkte

Nun schauen Sie sich nur die Schlagzeile, den Untertitel und das Bild zum Bericht an. Jetzt können Sie bereits eine genauere Aussage zum Inhalt machen.

Aufgabe 2

Complete the sentence below with the most suitable ending.

A woman knew how to save a man's life because she ...

- ☐ a once worked in a hospital.
- ☐ b had done a course on life-saving techniques.
- ☐ c saw what to do in a hospital series on television.
- ☐ d acts in a hospital series on television.

____ /1 Punkt

TV tactics help save man's life

Woman used techniques seen on TV programme *Casualty*

Gaye Knight was working in a photographic shop in Tunbridge Wells when one of the customers had a diabetic fit and collapsed. The customer, Richard Jarvis, stopped breathing and had no pulse. He had effectively died but Ms Knight resuscitated him and gave him heart massage which kept him alive till paramedics could take over.

Later, when one of the paramedics asked Ms Knight how she knew what to do, she said she remembered the techniques from a *Casualty* episode about diabetes. "I've spent hours glued to *Casualty*," she said. The stories take place in a fictional hospital's Accident and Emergency Department.

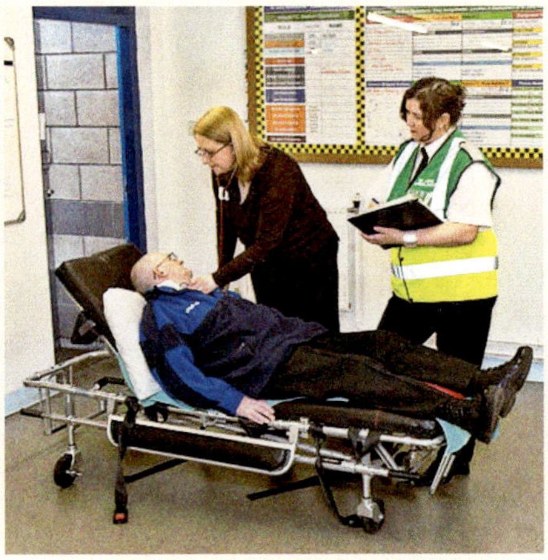

While waiting for the paramedics to arrive, Ms Knight thought about what she had seen on Casualty and did the same as the doctor in the series did there. She said: "The man was having a diabetic fit and soon afterwards it was obvious that he had gone into cardiac arrest and had stopped breathing. I felt for a pulse and there was no pulse so I started doing resuscitation on his chest and giving him heart massage."

Paramedic Tony Kemp paid tribute to Ms Knight and her actions. He said: "I was there within four or five minutes so the chances were fairly good that we could have restarted his heart. But those four to five minutes still take away some chance of survival. Gaye just got on and did it. She really saved his life."

Last week, Ms Knight was reunited with the man she helped save – now getting back to health – at the store where he collapsed. He said: "The last thing I remember was leaning against the wall and saying 'help me'. Then I came round in A and E."

Gaye said: "A lot of people laugh at these programmes, and I've actually watched a few episodes myself and thought 'this is unbelievable, does this really happen?'. But obviously it does happen."

320 words

Jetzt wissen Sie ungefähr, worum es im Text geht. Lesen Sie nun den vollständigen Zeitungsbericht. Behalten Sie dabei die Fragen von Aufgabe 1 im Hinterkopf.

adapted from: www.news.bbc.co.uk, 2 June, 2006

Aufgabe 3

Complete this summary with words or phrases from the text.

A woman was working in a ______________________[1] when a man ______________________[2]. The woman ______________________[3] the man and gave him ______________________[4]. She knew what to do because she ______________________[5] from a TV programme. A ______________________[6] who was called to the scene said that the woman had ______________________[7]. She said that she always watched *Casualty* on TV, but she sometimes thought it was ______________________[8].

Jetzt können Sie die erste grobe Zusammenfassung des Zeitungsberichts (Aufgabe 1) vervollständigen – auch wenn Sie vielleicht noch nicht wissen, was jedes Wort im Text bedeutet.

_____ /8 Punkte

PRACTICE 1

Zur Erinnerung: Die Schlagzeile weist auf den Textinhalt hin.

A Digitally 'replacing' Hollywood's stars

B Electronic key turns your Ford Focus into your Mom

C Online gamers 'are not unhealthy'

D Texting while driving 'worse than drinking'

E Facebook can ruin your life. And so can MySpace, Bebo …

F Computer games help social ties

Aufgabe 1

Which text is probably about …?

1 computer users who don't get enough exercise
2 problems with social networking websites
3 lonely computer users
4 cars that tell teenagers what to do
5 dangers of using mobile phones in cars
6 new developments in film-making

A	B	C	D	E	F

_____ / 6 Punkte

Vergessen Sie auch nicht, dass der erste und letzte Satz bzw. Absatz eines Textes oft die Aussage des Autors zusammenfasst.

Aufgabe 2

Here are six sentences from three different texts. Which are first sentences and which are last sentences? Match them to three of the headlines (A–F) above. The first sentence has been put in place for you.

1 A recent report says that, far from encouraging teenagers to be anti-social, video games help them engage with friends and community.
2 The "couch potato" image of computer gamers is unfounded, with many in better than average shape, claim US researchers in a new report.
3 People will post just about anything on social networking sites and the information can be used against them.
4 "Parents should look for games that offer their child opportunities to have more civically-minded experiences," the expert said in conclusion.
5 But if present trends continue and users fail to wise up, the sites might bring some unexpected shocks.
6 People talk about "gaming" as if it is always bad; they forget that there are fit gamers and unfit gamers – you just can't generalize.

[1] is a first sentence and [ ] is a last sentence. They are from text [ ].
[ ] is a first sentence and [ ] is a last sentence. They are from text [ ].
[ ] is a first sentence and [ ] is a last sentence. They are from text [ ].

_____ / 8 Punkte

Aufgabe 3

Match these lists of nouns (1–6) with the text headlines (A–F).

Zur Erinnerung: Schlüsselwörter geben Hinweise auf den Inhalt des Textes.

1 accident – parent – ignition key – ID chip
2 actor – action – computer – technology
3 friend – community – loner – real life
4 computer – gaming – exercise – lifestyle
5 employer – identity – information – privacy
6 alcohol – concentration – text message – motorist

A	B	C	D	E	F

____ / 6 Punkte

Aufgabe 4

Match these sentences to headlines A–F. In each sentence, underline at least two key words which helped you decide. One word in sentence 1 has been underlined for you.

Auch wenn Sie nicht jedes Wort verstehen, können Sie diese Sätze bestimmt dem jeweiligen Text zuordnen.

1 Adult gamers had a body mass index of just over 25, which is the threshold for "overweight", while the US average is 28.
2 Drivers face a £60 fine and three penalty points on their licence for using hand-held mobile phones while driving.
3 Being a player did not necessarily mean being a loner.
4 Employers and authorities are now monitoring what people believed were private websites – and using the contents against them.
5 Film-makers have used computer-generated visual effects to create space ships and monsters for some time.
6 It covers all the common parental complaints: The car's speed cannot exceed 80mph. Radio volume is limited to 44 percent of maximum, and, if seatbelts aren't fastened, no sound will come from the speakers at all.

A	B	C	D	E	F

____ / 6 Punkte

Extra-Aufgabe

Use the words from **Aufgabe 3** and the words you have underlined in **Aufgabe 4** to produce thematically-linked word lists (*Wortfelder*).

→ STEP 5: Learning vocabulary

Aufgabe 5

Cross out the incorrect adjective or adverb form.

Adjektive und Adverbien können ebenfalls wichtige Schlüsselwörter sein.

Scientists have developed new/newly [1] systems to make digital/digitally [2] doubles of actors which look so real/really [3] that audiences will never notice the difference. The process begins with an extreme/extremely [4] high-tech photograph. A camera has been special/specially [5] developed to scan an actor's face in extraordinary/extraordinarily [6] detail. The data is then used on a computer to digital/digitally [7] manipulate the image. Amazing/Amazingly [8], film-makers can create incredible/incredibly [9] action sequences, featuring the actor, which never actual/actually [10] happened. Does this sound unbelievable/unbelievably [11]? No, they are complete/completely [12] convincing. But the technology is not designed to replace humans entire/entirely [13]. It will be used to re-shoot scenes when the actor has moved on to another project or has changed their physical/physically [14] appearance.

REMEMBER!

Adjektiv oder Adverb
- Adjektive beschreiben Personen oder Sachen näher.
- Nach Verben wie *be, feel, look, sound, smell* und *taste* werden Adjektive verwendet.
- Adjektiv + *-ly* = Adverb. (Unregelmäßige Adverbien muss man lernen.)
- Adverbien beschreiben Verben näher.
- Adverbien beschreiben auch Adjektive, andere Adverbien oder ganze Sätze näher.

____ / 14 Punkte

Ich habe ____ Minuten für diesen Abschnitt gebraucht.

Ich habe ____ Mal ein Wörterbuch verwendet.

Ich habe ____ von 55 Punkten.

Jetzt kontrollieren Sie alle Antworten im Lösungsheft auf Seite 2.

Reading Skills 2: Dealing with unknown words
Topics: Media, Society

Konnten Sie alle Fragen in Step 1, Aufgabe 3 (Seite 3) beantworten? Oder fehlen ein paar Einzelheiten? Dann macht das eine oder andere Wort wahrscheinlich doch noch Schwierigkeiten. Deshalb werden wir uns nun die unbekannten Wörter aus dem Text **TV tactics help save man's life** genauer anschauen.

Dealing with unknown words

In jedem neuen Text werden Sie mit Wörtern konfrontiert, die Sie noch nicht kennen. Hier ein paar Tipps, wie Sie mit diesen Wörtern leichter umgehen können.

- Viele Wörter sind **in fast allen Sprachen** der Welt **gleich**; dies gilt besonders für Begriffe aus den Bereichen Medien, Wirtschaft und Technik, z. B. *star*, *marketing*, *computer*.
- Andere englische Wörter sind **mit deutschen Begriffen verwandt**, z. B. *friend/Freund*, *house/Haus*, oder sie stammen von den gleichen Fremdwörtern ab, z. B. *aggressive/aggressiv*, *democracy/Demokratie*.
- Versuchen Sie, die Bedeutung **aus dem Zusammenhang** (*context*) heraus zu erschließen. Wenn Sie den Text insgesamt betrachten, was könnte das Wort dann bedeuten? Welche Hinweise gibt der Satz/Absatz, in dem das Wort vorkommt?
- Viele Wörter kann man **am Wortstamm erkennen**, z. B. *agree/disagree*, *happy/happiness*. (→ **Anhang 1:** Wordbuilding, S. 54)
- Greifen Sie nur dann zum **Wörterbuch**, wenn alle anderen Herleitungsversuche fehlgeschlagen sind. (→ STEP 4: Using a dictionary, S. 14)

Sie wissen jetzt, wovon der Text handelt. Bei Aufgabe 1 geht es um spezifische Wörter, die Sie entweder auf Deutsch kennen oder aus dem Zusammenhang erschließen können.

Aufgabe 1

First, find English words in the text on page 3 that match the German words (1–5) below. Make a note of the line number where you found the word.

1 Diabetes ______________________ line ____

2 kollabieren ______________________ line ____

3 Puls ______________________ line ____

4 Herzmassage ______________________ line ____

5 im Effekt ______________________ line ____

Now match the English words (6–10) with their German translations (a–e).

6	fit (line 4)	a	Rettungssanitäter/in
7	cardiac arrest (line 24)	b	Überleben
8	resuscitation (line 27)	c	Anfall
9	paramedic (line 29)	d	Wiederbelebung
10	survival (line 35)	e	Herzinfarkt

____ / 10 Punkte

Jetzt beschäftigen wir uns mit dem Thema Wortbildung.

Aufgabe 2

Find the following words in the text. Make a note of the line number where you found the word.

1 the adjective form of "diabetes" ______________________ line ____

2 the verb form of "resuscitation" ______________________ line ____

3 a verb meaning "to get something going again" ______________________ line ____

4 a verb meaning "to bring two people together again" ______________________ line ____

5 an adjective meaning "*unglaubhaft*" ______________________ line ____

REMEMBER!

Die Vorsilben *re-* und *un-*
- Die Vorsilbe *re-* bedeutet „nochmal".
- Die Vorsilbe *un-* bedeutet (wie im Deutschen) „nicht".

____ / 5 Punkte

Aufgabe 3

Find adverbs in the text with the following meanings. Make a note of the line number where you found the word.

1 ziemlich ______________________ line ____
2 wirklich ______________________ line ____
3 tatsächlich ______________________ line ____
4 offensichtlich ______________________ line ____

____ / 4 Punkte

Aufgabe 4

Tick (✓) the most suitable answer.

Es gibt nicht nur einzelne Wörter, die unbekannt oder problematisch sind. Auch Redewendungen können Kopfzerbrechen verursachen. Aber mit Ihrem Wissen zum Text können Sie die nächste Aufgabe leicht lösen.

1 "I've spent hours glued to *Casualty*." (lines 13–14) means that Ms Knight …
  a has been waiting in hospital for hours. ☐
  b enjoys watching *Casualty* on TV. ☐
  c has worked in a hospital for some years. ☐
  d hates watching *Casualty* on TV. ☐

2 "He had gone into cardiac arrest." (line 24) means that …
  a Mr Jarvis had stopped breathing. ☐
  b he had collapsed. ☐
  c Mr Jarvis' heart had stopped beating. ☐
  d he had lain down to have a rest. ☐

3 "Tony Kemp paid tribute to Ms Knight." (lines 29–30) means that he …
  a said that Ms Knight had done a good job. ☐
  b thanked Ms Knight. ☐
  c gave Ms Knight some money. ☐
  d complained about Ms Knight. ☐

4 "Gaye just got on and did it." (lines 35–36) means that she …
  a rang for an ambulance first. ☐
  b waited until the paramedic arrived. ☐
  c started to help the man immediately. ☐
  d went to hospital with Mr Jarvis. ☐

5 "Then I came round in A and E." (lines 42–43) means "Then I …
  a went to hospital." ☐
  b arrived at the hospital." ☐
  c got back home." ☐
  d woke up in hospital." ☐

____ / 5 Punkte

(idiom) **to be glued to sth** = an etwas kleben

Ein Idiom ist ein Ausdruck, dessen Bedeutung nicht mit Hilfe des regulären Wortschatzes bestimmt werden kann. Wörter haben innerhalb des Ausdrucks eine andere Bedeutung als in freier Verwendung. → STEP 4

PRACTICE 2

Erinnern Sie sich: In den Bereichen Medien und Technik gibt es sehr viele international gebräuchliche Begriffe oder ähnliche Ausdrücke. Man muss aber nicht immer beim nächstbesten Wort bleiben. Manchmal lohnt es sich, etwas freier zu kombinieren.

Bearbeiten Sie jetzt die Aufgaben 1 und 2.

Digitally 'replacing' Hollywood's stars
The data is used on a computer to manipulate the image. The film-maker can create an action sequence, featuring the "actor", which never actually happened. But for the film fan the feeling is just the same.

Aufgabe 1

First, complete the middle column with "international" or similar (= *ähnlich*) words to the underlined words in the text above. Then add another German word which has the same meaning. The first word has been done for you.

	Words in the text	International words/ similar German words	Other German words
1	data	Daten	Informationen
2	computer		
3	manipulate		
4	image		
5	film-maker		
6	create		
7	action		
8	sequence		
9	fan		
10	feeling		

____ / 18 Punkte

Aufgabe 2

Es ist eine große Hilfe beim Textverständnis, wenn Sie Wortbildungen bzw. Wortarten vom Stammwort ableiten können. Schlagen Sie die Informationen zur Wortbildung nach (→ **Anhang 1**, S. 54) und bearbeiten Sie dann die Aufgaben 2 und 3.

Make adjectives from the words in the box and complete the table and headings.

nouns: anger • education • health • industry • power • success
verbs: advise • change • create • manage • progress • support

Adjectives formed from ...		
-al	*-y*	*-ful*
educational		

Adjectives formed from ...	
-ive	*-able*

____ / 13 Punkte

Aufgabe 3

Make nouns from the words in the box and complete the table and headings.

agree • create • creative • educate • employ • fair • happy • ill • imagine • manage • productive • stupid

Nouns formed from ...		Nouns formed from ...	
-(a)tion	*-ment*	*-ity*	*-ness*
creation			

____ / 14 Punkte

Aufgabe 4

Complete the text with the opposite of the word in brackets. Use your dictionary if you're not sure of the answer.

Edit Blog Entry | Preview Blog Entry | Links | User (2)

It's ______________________[1] (credible) what some people post on their social networking websites. They seem to think that it's ______________________[2] (likely) there will be any problems. Bad things happening to a blogger may be ______________________[3] (probable), but they're definitely not ______________________[4] (possible). In some cases a blogger may find themselves in the ______________________[5] (pleasant) position of having to explain the ______________________[6] (polite) things they wrote about their ______________________[7] (popular) employer in their weblog. And the worst thing is, the World Wide Web does not forget and bloggers will be ______________________[8] (successful) if they want to remove what they've posted later. Some of the things you find on these sites may simply be stupid, ______________________[9] (responsible) or just ______________________[10] (agreeable), but you'll also find blogs that contain things that are ______________________[11] (honest) or even ______________________[12] (legal).

REMEMBER!

Adjektive und ihr Gegenteil
Zu den meisten Adjektiven bildet man das Gegenteil mit einer der Vorsilben *un-*, *in-* oder *dis-*. Bei Adjektiven, die mit *c*, *l*, *m*, *p* oder *r* anfangen wird das Gegenteil mit *in-*, *il-*, *im-* oder *ir-* gebildet.

____ / 12 Punkte

Ich habe ____ Minuten für diesen Abschnitt gebraucht.

Ich habe ____ Mal ein Wörterbuch verwendet.

Ich habe ____ von 81 Punkten.

Jetzt kontrollieren Sie alle Antworten im Lösungsheft auf den Seiten 2–4.

STEP 3

Reading Skills 3: Reading for detail / "Scanning"
Topics: Free time, Media

Sie werden nicht nur nach dem allgemeinen Sinn eines Textes gefragt werden, sondern müssen auch konkrete Fragen zu Details beantworten können.

Aber wie schafft man das, ohne bei jeder Frage den ganzen Text noch einmal durchlesen zu müssen?

Scanning for information

Folgen Sie diesen Schritten, um schnell und effektiv Informationen zu sammeln.

- **Fragen lesen:** Schauen Sie sich die Fragen an, die konkrete Details aus dem Text verlangen, und vergewissern Sie sich, dass Sie die Frage(n) richtig verstehen.
- **Text lesen:** Lesen Sie den Text zügig und ohne anzuhalten durch, um den allgemeinen Sinn zu erfassen. (→ STEP 1)
- **Schlüsselwörter suchen:** Merken Sie sich die *key words*, die in den Fragen verwendet werden. Suchen Sie diese Ausdrücke jetzt im Text: Lassen Sie dabei die Augen über den Text gleiten – die gesuchten Wörter werden Ihnen ins Auge springen!
- **Fragen den Absätzen zuordnen:** Die Fragen kommen meistens in derselben Reihenfolge wie die Informationen im Text.
- **Informationen notieren:** Wenn Sie die richtige Textstelle gefunden haben, markieren oder notieren Sie die Details, die Sie brauchen.
- **Unbekannte Wörter behandeln:** Schauen Sie unbekannte Wörter nur im Wörterbuch nach, wenn das zur Beantwortung der Frage unbedingt notwendig ist. (→ STEP 2)
- **Text noch einmal lesen:** Lesen Sie zumindest die von Ihnen gefundene Textstelle noch einmal durch, um sicher zu gehen, dass Sie keine Details übersehen haben.
- **Antwort schreiben:** Benutzen Sie Ihre Notizen/Markierungen, um die Aufgabe zu bearbeiten.

Lesen Sie nun Aufgabe 1 und dann den folgenden Text und beantworten Sie die Aufgabe.

REMEMBER!

Mobile phone vs. Cellphone

- BE = mobile (phone)
- AE = cellphone / cellular phone

Tipp! Nur weil ein **key word** in einem Absatz vorkommt, bedeutet das nicht unbedingt, dass Sie das Thema des Absatzes bereits gefunden haben. Lesen Sie weiter, um sicher zu gehen.

Hi-tech brings families together

Technology is helping families stay in touch like never before, says a report.

A Instead of driving people apart, mobile phones and the net are helping them maintain social ties, says the Pew Internet report. Families are also among the keenest users of technology, the survey of 2,252 Americans revealed. It found that using the net was often a social activity within families, with 51% of parents saying they browsed the web with their children. "Some analysts have worried that new technologies hurt family togetherness, but we see that technology allows for new kinds of connectedness built around cellphones and the internet," said Tracy Kennedy of the University of Toronto who helped to write the Networked Families report.

B The research looked at the differences in technology use between families with children and single adults, couples without children and adults who share a home but are not related. It found that traditional so-called "nuclear" families were more likely to have more hi-tech gadgetry in their home than almost any other group it measured. Multiple mobile phones were found in 89% of nuclear families and 66% had a high-speed net connection. The US national average for broadband is 52%. It also found that 58% of this type of family were likely to have more than two computers in the home.

C Many people use their mobile phone to keep in touch and maintain social ties with parents, siblings and children. Seventy percent of couples who both own a mobile use it every day to chat or say hello. In addition, 42% of parents contact their children via their mobile every day. This led to 53% of those questioned saying that new technologies had increased the quality of their contact with distant family members, while 47% said it improved interaction with those they live with.

D The growing use of cellphones, computers and the net meant that families no longer gathered round the TV for shared experiences but, according to the report, this did not mean that these communal times had vanished. Instead, the report found that 52% of net users who live with their partner and have children go online in the company of someone else several times a week. For many, greater use of the net came at the expense of TV watching, with 25% saying they now spent less time watching television. Only 58% of 18–29 year olds said they watched TV every day.

402 words

adapted from: www.news.bbc.co.uk, 20 October, 2008

Aufgabe 1

Match these key words to the paragraphs in the text.

1 nuclear families ☐
3 watching TV ☐
2 social ties ☐
4 mobile phones ☐

___ /4 Punkte

Aufgabe 2

Multiple choice: Choose the most suitable option.

Mit Aufgabe 1 haben Sie den Absätzen Themenbereiche zugeordnet. Bearbeiten Sie jetzt Aufgabe 2. Lesen Sie zuerst alle Fragen durch und überlegen Sie, in welchem Absatz die Information zu finden sein wird.

1 According to the text, which new technologies are helping to keep families together?
   a internet and TV
   b mobile phones and internet
   c mobile phones and TV
   d computers and TV

2 Which family group is more likely to have high-tech gadgetry in their home?
   a parents with children
   b adults who live on their own
   c married couples who have no children
   d friends who live together

3 How many people on average have a high-speed internet connection in America?
   a 9 out of 10
   b about two-thirds
   c about half
   d about a third

4 What percentage of couples talk to each other on their mobile phones every day?
   a 70%
   b 53%
   c 47%
   d 42%

5 The research showed that because they used the internet more, ...
   a only 25% of people now watch TV.
   b only 18–29 year olds watch TV.
   c people watch TV every day.
   d 25% of people watch less TV.

1	2	3	4	5

___ /5 Punkte

Aufgabe 3

Without looking at your dictionary, try to work out the meaning of these words as they are used in the text.

1 togetherness (line 12) ____________________

2 connectedness (line 13) ____________________

3 gadgetry (line 25) ____________________

4 sibling (line 35) ____________________

___ /4 Punkte

Auch dieser Zeitungsartikel befasst sich mit der Umfrage zu Internet-Gewohnheiten. Nachdem Sie die Aufgaben 1–3 angeschaut haben, lesen Sie den Text, und dann bearbeiten Sie die Aufgaben. Sie müssen nicht jedes Wort verstehen, um die Fragen zu beantworten.

Computer games drive social ties

Far from turning teenagers into anti-social loners, video games help them engage with friends and community, says a report.

A The Pew Internet study of US teenagers found that few play alone and most join up with friends when gaming. It found that many used educational games to learn about world issues and to begin to engage with politics. The report also found that gaming had become an almost universal pastime among young Americans.

B The survey of 1,102 teenagers aged 12–17 revealed that 99% of boys and 94% of girls across the socio-economic spectrum play some kind of computer or video game. The most popular title was *Guitar Hero*, followed by *Halo 3*, *Madden NFL*, *Solitaire*, and *Dance Dance Revolution*. Most teenagers played a variety of different titles, said Amanda Lenhart, senior research specialist at the Pew Internet & American Life Project, who wrote the report. "They range in terms of their content from things that are about solving problems to things that are about going out and shooting things, or driving things, or racing things, or playing a sport," Ms Lenhart said.

C Computer games have been linked in media reports and recent research with anti-social behaviour – particularly among young men between the ages of 15 and 25. There is always the danger that excessive gaming can lead to addiction, social isolation and, in extreme cases, violence against other members of society.

D But, Ms Lenhart argued, being a player did not always mean being a loner. "Three quarters of teens actually play these games with other people, whether online or in person." Even playing games every day does not appear to impact teenagers' social lives. "People who game on a daily basis are just as likely to talk on the phone, to email or to spend time with a friend face to face outside of school as kids who play games less," she said.

E It was also a mistake to think that video and computer games were divorced from real life, she added. The study found that 52% of the teenagers played games that involved thinking about moral and ethical issues, 43% played games in which they made decisions about how a community, city or nation should be run, and 40% played games where they learned about a social issue. This included specifically educational titles such as *The Food Force* and *Darfur is Dying*, but also more mainstream games such as *Civilization*. Teenagers who were forced to confront problems in virtual communities were more likely to raise money for charity, volunteer, stay informed about political issues, persuade others to vote or march in a protest or demonstration.

F Ms Lenhart said the report revealed that the amount of time spent playing computer games didn't dent the amount of community engagement the teenagers took part in, but that teenagers who played with other people in person did tend to be more engaged with their communities. "What we say to parents is, pay attention to the games that your child is playing, see what they do in the games, and look for games that offer your child opportunities to have more civically-minded experiences," she said.

481 words

adapted from: www.news.bbc.co.uk, 16 June, 2008

Aufgabe 1

Multiple matching: Match the headings 1–8 to the paragraphs A–F. There are two more headings than you need.

1 Players not always alone
2 Gaming – a favourite pastime
3 Games too expensive
4 Games can have social content
5 Advice for parents
6 Negative aspects of gaming
7 Too many violent games
8 Different types of games

A	B	C	D	E	F

____ / 6 Punkte

Aufgabe 2

Short answer questions: Answer the following questions. Short phrases will do.

1 How many boys and how many girls play some sort of video game?

____

2 Which computer game is played the most?

____

3 What do computer games offer apart from shooting, driving or racing things?

____

4 What three things do teenagers still do, even though they spend time gaming?

____

5 What would people have to think about in a game like *Civilization*?

____

6 What is the purpose of games such as *The Food Force* or *Darfur is Dying?*

____

____ / 10 Punkte

Aufgabe 3

Gapped summary: Fill in the blanks with words from the text. The missing words are in the same order as in the text.

A recent ____________[1] has found that computer ____________[2] is a very popular ____________[3] among US teenagers. There are obvious dangers to ____________[4] gaming, such as ____________[5], social isolation and even ____________[6]. However, 75% of teenagers play with someone else, either ____________[7] or in person. Some experts think that teenagers can learn about social ____________[8] from ____________[9] games or games that force them to ____________[10] real problems in ____________[11] communities. The author of the report advises ____________[12] to pay ____________[13] to the games their children play.

____ / 13 Punkte

Ich habe ____ Minuten für diesen Abschnitt gebraucht.

Ich habe ____ Mal ein Wörterbuch verwendet.

Ich habe ____ von 42 Punkten.

Jetzt kontrollieren Sie alle Antworten im Lösungsheft auf Seite 4.

Die wichtigste Frage, die Sie sich beim Benutzen eines Wörterbuchs stellen können, lautet: „Muss ich dieses Wort überhaupt nachschlagen?"

Using a monolingual dictionary

Wenn Sie beim Lesen eines Textes die folgenden sechs Fragen mit „nein" beantworten können, dürfen Sie zum Wörterbuch greifen:

1 Ist es ein **allseits gebräuchlicher Begriff**, wie z. B. *marketing*?
2 Kenne ich ein **ähnliches deutsches Wort**?
3 Gibt es ein **ähnliches Fremdwort**, wie z. B. *democracy/Demokratie*?
4 Kann ich das Wort **vom Wortstamm ableiten**?
5 Ist die Bedeutung des Wortes **aus dem Zusammenhang** des Texts (*context*) **erkennbar**?
6 Kann ich den Text bzw. die Fragen zum Text **verstehen**, **ohne die Bedeutung des Wortes** zu wissen?

Lesen Sie – ohne Wörterbuch! – diesen kurzen Textausschnitt, in dem ein Radfahrer sich über andere Verkehrsteilnehmer beschwert. Dann bearbeiten Sie Aufgabe 1.

What do you think would be the greatest danger to cyclists as they pedal around the roads of a busy city? Trucks, motorbikes, bendy buses, perhaps? This might sound a bit like nonsense, but for me, the biggest problem – and without doubt, the biggest menace – are pedestrians. Since the proliferation of the iPod, they are more likely than any other moving object to inadvertently place themselves directly in my path while I'm cycling, forcing me either to brake suddenly or to swerve out into the traffic – and both of these actions could make me or someone else end up in a nasty accident.

103 words

adapted from: www.independent.co.uk, 7 August, 2008

Aufgabe 1

______ / 26 Punkte

Complete the table. Only use your dictionary if you really need to.

Which question from the Skill box can I answer with yes?		Comments	Word class (Wortart)	Definition	German
pedal	Nr. 2	*Pedal* (German noun)	verb	to turn or press the pedals on a bicycle	
traffic	5	—			
nonsense	3	*Nonsens*		ideas, ...	
menace	—	—		sth that may cause ...	
pedestrian	5	use iPods, not in trucks, not on motorbikes, etc.			
proliferation	—	—			
inadvertently	6	—			
brake	4 + 5	brake (n); see swerve			
swerve	5	sth you do on a bike to avoid an accident			
nasty	5 (6)	sth to do with an accident			

Aufgabe 2

Answer these questions on the two dictionary entries below.

1 What is a synonym for 'menace' as it is used in the text (line 7)?

____

2 Which three collocations are given for 'menace'?

____

3 What is a synonym for the verb form of 'menace'?

____

4 Give the adjective and adverb forms of 'menace'.

____

5 Say which two word classes (parts of speech) 'traffic' can be.

____

6 Give five collocations of 'traffic'.

____

____ / 14 Punkte

Headword: correct spelling and hyphenation (**Silbentrennung**)

Word class: noun, verb, adjective, etc.

men *pl.* of MAN

men·ace /'menəs/ *noun, verb*

■ ***noun*** **1** [C, usually sing.] **~ (to sb/sth)** a person or thing that causes, or may cause, serious damage, harm or danger SYN THREAT: *a new initiative aimed at beating the menace of illegal drugs* **2** [U] an atmosphere that makes you feel threatened or frightened: ***a sense/an air/a hint of menace*** *in his voice* **3** [C, usually sing.] (*informal*) a person or thing that is annoying or causes trouble SYN NUISANCE **4 menaces** [pl.] (*BrE, law*) threats that sb will cause harm if they do not get what they are asking for: *to demand money* ***with menaces***

■ ***verb*** [VN] (*formal*) to be a possible danger to sth/sb SYN THREATEN: *The forests are being menaced by major development projects.*

men·acing /'menəsɪŋ/ *adj.* seeming likely to cause you harm or danger SYN THREATENING: *a* ***menacing face/tone*** ◇ *At night, the dark streets become menacing.* ▶ **men·acing·ly** *adv.*: *The thunder growled menacingly.*

mé·nage /meɪ'nɑːʒ/ *noun* [usually sing.] (from *French, formal* or *humorous*) all the people who live together in one house SYN HOUSEHOLD

Definition: meaning of the word, usually with an example sentence

Register: formal, informal, slang, etc.

Synonyms: words of similar meaning

Example sentence

Derivatives: words from the same word family

Grammatical information: whether a noun is countable (C) or uncountable (U), whether a verb can take an object or not

Pronunciation: correct pronunciation (**Aussprache**) and stress (**Betonung**)

traf·fic /'træfɪk/ *noun, verb*

■ ***noun*** [U] **1** the vehicles that are on a road at a particular time: ***heavy/rush-hour traffic*** ◇ ***local/through traffic*** ◇ *There's always a lot of traffic at this time of day.* ◇ *They were stuck* ***in traffic*** *and missed their flight.* ◇ *a plan to reduce* ***traffic congestion*** ◇ ***traffic police*** (= who control traffic on a road or stop drivers who are breaking the law) ◇ *The delay is due simply to the* ***volume of traffic***. **2** the movement of ships, trains, aircraft, etc. along a particular route: *transatlantic traffic* ◇ *air traffic control* **3** the movement of people or goods from one place to another: ***commuter/freight/passenger traffic*** ◇ *the traffic of goods between one country and another* **4** the movement of messages and signals through an electronic communication system: *the computer servers that manage global Internet traffic* **5 ~ (in sth)** illegal trade in sth: *the traffic in firearms*

■ ***verb*** (-ck-) PHR V **'traffic in sth** to buy and sell sth illegally: *to traffic in drugs* ▶ **traf·fick·er** *noun*: *a drugs trafficker* **traf·fick·ing** *noun* [U]: *drug trafficking*

Collocations: words that often are used with the headword

Forms: unusual plural, participle or -ing forms

Phrasal verbs or idioms

Lesen Sie den Textausschnitt von Seite 14 weiter und bearbeiten Sie die Aufgaben 1–3.

But since the proliferation of digital music players, an increasing number of people walk around in a complete daze – stepping into cycle lanes, walking out from behind stationary vehicles and crossing roads without so much as a turn of the head, to check if something is coming.

I've no doubt my agitation is somewhat disproportionate. After all, I've not yet actually come off my bike as a result of an absent-minded walker. But what makes me so frustrated is that pedestrians don't seem to consider bicycles to be any great threat to them. While you'll often see people running across the road when they see a car coming, they often seem totally nonchalant when a bike hurtles towards them.

119 words

adapted from: www.independent.co.uk, 7 August, 2008

Aufgabe 1

Look at these dictionary entries and answer the questions.

agi·ta·tion /ˌædʒɪˈteɪʃn/ *noun* **1** [U] worry and anxiety that you show by behaving in a nervous way: *Dot arrived in a state of great agitation.* **2** [U, C] ~ **(for/against sth)** public protest in order to achieve political change: *widespread agitation for social reform* **3** [U] (*technical*) the act of stirring or shaking a liquid

non·cha·lant /ˈnɒnʃələnt; *NAmE* ˌnɑːnʃəˈlɑːnt/ *adj.* behaving in a calm and relaxed way; giving the impression that you are not feeling any anxiety SYN CASUAL: *to* ***appear/look/sound nonchalant*** ◇ *'It'll be fine,' she replied, with a nonchalant shrug.* ▶ **non·cha·lance** /-ləns; *NAmE* -ˈlɑːns/ *noun* [U]: *an air of nonchalance* **non·cha·lant·ly** *adv.*: *He was leaning nonchalantly against the wall.*

ˌabsent-ˈminded *adj.* tending to forget things, perhaps because you are not thinking about what is around you, but about sth else SYN FORGETFUL ▶ **ˌabsent-ˈminded·ly** *adv.* **ˌabsent-ˈminded·ness** *noun* [U]

hur·tle /ˈhɜːtl; *NAmE* ˈhɜːrtl/ *verb* [V + *adv./prep.*] to move very fast in a particular direction: *A runaway car* ***came hurtling*** *towards us.*

1 Which meaning of 'agitation' is used in the text (line 9)?

____

2 Is 'agitation' used in the text as a countable or as an uncountable noun?

____

3 Give a synonym for 'absent-minded' (line 12). ______________

4 What are the adverb and noun forms of 'absent-minded'?

____

5 What is the noun form of 'nonchalant' (line 18)? ______________

6 Rewrite this sentence, using a synonym: 'He was leaning <u>nonchalantly</u> against the wall.'

____

7 Rewrite this sentence using a collocation of 'hurtle' (line 18): 'The bike <u>hurtled</u> towards them.'

____

____ /8 Punkte

Aufgabe 2

Use an English-English dictionary to find the answer to these questions.

1 What idiom does 'daze' (line 3) occur in? ______________

2 What is the opposite of 'stationary' (line 5)? ______________

3 Find a word that is almost the same as 'stationary' and is pronounced exactly the same way. What does it mean? ______________

4 What is the opposite of 'disproportionate'? ______________

5 Near to 'disproportionate' find one noun, one verb and one other adjective that builds its opposite in the same way. ______________

→ **Anhang 1:** Word building, S. 54

____ /8 Punkte

Aufgabe 3

Look up the word 'turn' in your English-English dictionary and answer these questions.

1 What part of speech is the 'turn' as used in the text (line 6)? How would you translate it into German? ______________________

2 How would you translate 'turn' in these idioms?

a a good turn ______________________

b in turns ______________________

c the turn of the century ______________________

d a turn of the screw ______________________

____ / 6 Punkte

Aufgabe 4

Use the words from the box to make phrasal verbs.

about • around • for • forward to • off (3 x) • on (2 x) • on with • out (3 x) • to • up (6 x) • up with

I have given _up_ 1 cycling to work, because the rush-hour traffic is too dangerous. But what can I do instead? The oil companies keep putting ________ 2 the price of petrol, so cars are too expensive, and the buses are always late. Then I heard ________ 3 a new idea: sharing a taxi with other people. I looked it ________ 4 on the internet and found ________ 5 all the details. You just have to wait ________ 6 them to pick you ________ 7 at home and then you tell them where you want to go. I was really looking ________ 8 it. But it turned ________ 9 not to be such a good idea after all. On the first day I waited an hour before a little minibus turned ________ 10 and then I had to put ________ 11 all the other passengers inside. I found it really hard to get ________ 12 them. I pointed ________ 13 to them that I was in a hurry when we set ________ 14, but they just carried ________ 15 talking ________ 16 the driver as he crawled from one stop to another. In the end, I had to call ________ 17 the whole idea and get ________ 18 a bus. Of course, it was crowded, too, and by the time I had got ________ 19 near the office it was almost time to turn ________ 20 and go home. I'm going to have to think ________ 21 a new plan soon.

Phrasal verbs bestehen aus **verb + preposition**. Die Bedeutung ist oft ganz anders als beim Stammverb.
→ **Anhang 3**: Phrasal verbs, S. 55

____ / 20 Punkte

Ich habe ____ Minuten für diesen Abschnitt gebraucht.

Ich habe ____ Mal ein Wörterbuch verwendet.

Ich habe ____ von 82 Punkten.

Jetzt kontrollieren Sie alle Antworten im Lösungsheft auf den Seiten 5/6.

STEP 5

Vocabulary Skills 2: Learning vocabulary effectively
Topics: The world of work, Migrant workers; Youth culture, Music

In der Oberstufe werden Sie oft Texte als Kopien bekommen oder aus dem Internet herunterladen. Da werden die Vokabeln nicht immer so schön in Wörterverzeichnissen aufbereitet sein, wie Sie es bis jetzt von Ihren Schulbüchern gewohnt waren. Wie können Sie Ihre Wortschatzkenntnisse trotzdem systematisch ausbauen?

Learning vocabulary effectively

Wenn Sie effektiv mit Vokabeln arbeiten wollen, sollten Sie versuchen, möglichst viele Verbindungen zwischen den Wörtern aufzubauen. Sie werden dabei merken, dass die neuen Vokabeln viel fester im Gedächtnis verankert bleiben, und Sie können den aktiv benötigten Wortschatz viel leichter abrufen. Mit diesen Techniken schaffen Sie bessere Verbindungen zwischen den Wörtern:

- **Wortfamilien sammeln:** Vokabeln in Wortfamilien zu lernen kann sehr nützlich sein, wenn man mit unbekannten Wörtern konfrontiert wird (→ STEP 2). Mit den Wortfamilien sollten Sie auch *synonyms* und *opposites* sammeln.
- **Wortkombinationen sammeln:** Viele Wörter verwendet man oft in feststehenden Begriffen (*collocations*), z. B. *get rid of* / „loswerden" oder in *Verb-Noun*-Verbindungen, z. B. *handle a problem* / „ein Problem in den Griff bekommen". Ein gutes einsprachiges Wörterbuch gibt Hinweise zum Gebrauch eines Begriffs in Kombination mit anderen Wörtern (→ STEP 4).
- **Wortfelder sammeln:** Wörter zu einem bestimmten Thema lassen sich gut in Form eines Wortnetzes visuell darstellen. Vorteil: Man kann sie in Untergruppen gliedern, und die Liste ist unbegrenzt erweiterbar.

Lesen Sie nun den Text und bearbeiten Sie die Aufgaben. Machen Sie sich keine Sorgen, wenn Sie nicht jedes Wort verstehen; Sie werden sich mit diesem Text in → STEP 6 ausführlich beschäftigen.

Poles Apart

By **Carla Power**

A Since the European Union's enlargement in 2004, when Britain opened its job market to Europe's new member states, Poles have provided the British economy with a flood of cheap labour. The immigration wave took Britain by surprise. While the government expected at most 13,000 East Europeans annually, nearly 800,000 applied for work permits between 2004 and the end of 2007. The stereotypical arrival was the Polish plumber, but thousands of professionals arrived too.

B Now, though, many Polish workers are returning home or seeking jobs in Sweden or Norway, or France (where salaries are paid in the soaring euro). "They can't find work here, and they came to work, not to get job benefits," says Jan Mokrzycki, president of the Federation of Poles in Great Britain. Earlier this summer, the Polish daily *Dziennik Zwiazkowy* reported that job offers for Poles in the UK and Ireland were down a third on last year, and a recent report estimated that about half of the million East Europeans who arrived since enlargement in 2004 have left. The Polish consulate in London expects about 300,000 to 400,000 Poles to remain in Britain – still a huge number to have settled in just a few years. "A lot of these migrants were not coming to build a new life for themselves," says Philip Whyte of the Centre for European Reform. "They were coming to get a financial leg-up."

C Financial considerations are now driving them home again. In Poland, wages rose 7.7% last year, double their growth rate in the UK; and Poland's unemployment rate has dropped from about 14% to under 10% in two years. Newly arrived Poles, eager for jobs, were willing to work for low wages. The influx of Poles triggered tabloid scare stories about Polish labourers stealing jobs and soaking up social services. Now their departure has stirred doleful speculation about labour shortages: GET YOUR TAPS FIXED WHILE YOU CAN, warned a headline in the *Times* of London.

D With the Polish economy growing at over 6%, there's a steady campaign to lure foreign workers home. Polish newspapers in Britain run ads from companies in Poland looking for returnee workers; builders are particularly in demand as the country pours money into infrastructure for the 2012 European Football Championship. Polish employers have trekked out to London job fairs looking for labour, while the city of Wroclaw even mounted its own campaign, sending officials to Britain to encourage Poles to return.

E "People who work abroad are perceived in Poland as very rich and successful," says *Polish Times* editor Katarzyna Kopacz. "But many of them suffer poverty, with only part-time jobs and growing debts." As the economy turns sour in Britain, you can expect many more Poles to head for where the job opportunities lie: home.

457 words

adapted from: www.time.com, 4 September, 2008

Aufgabe 1

Complete the missing details from this index card. Use your dictionary if necessary.

employ

verb	**noun (person)**	**noun (abstract)**	**adjective**
employ	______________	______________	______________
	______________		______________

opposites: ______________ ; unemployed; unemployable

collocation: ______________ agency

synonyms: employee = worker, labourer (BE), laborer (AE)

verb	**noun (person)**	**noun (abstract)**	**adjective**
______________	worker	______________	______________
______________	labourer	______________	

Wortfamilien und Wortkombinationen können entweder in Listen oder auf Karteikarten gesammelt werden. Karteikarten eignen sich besonders gut zum Lernen. Sie können die deutschen Begriffe auf die Rückseite schreiben, um sich leichter testen zu können.

____ / 12 Punkte

Extra-Aufgabe

You can use the details from the card above to produce your own index card. The reverse side has been started for you.

beschäftigen / Arbeit geben

Verb	**Substantiv (Person)**	**Substantiv (abstrakt)**	**Adjektiv**
beschäftigen	Arbeitgeber/in Arbeitnehmer/in	Beschäftigung	beschäftigt anstellbar

Es lohnt sich, jede Art von Wortkombination (**collocation**) zu lernen. Diese können Sie entweder in übersichtlichen Listen schreiben, oder Sie ergänzen Ihre Karteikarten damit.

Aufgabe 2

Complete the missing items in the list and on the index card with collocations from the text.

job collocations			
(compound nouns)		(verb)	______ a job (*Arbeit suchen*)
job ______	(*Arbeitsmarkt*)	(verb + prep)	______ a job (*Arbeit suchen*)
job ______	(*Arbeitslosengeld*)		
job ______	(*Jobangebot*)	(adj)	full-time job (*Vollzeitjob*)
job ______	(*Jobmesse*)	(adj)	______ job (*Teilzeitjob*)
job ______	(*Arbeitsmöglichkeit*)	(adj + prep)	______ a job (*arbeitswillig*)

Schlagen Sie die Begriffe „job" und „work" in Ihrem einsprachigen Wörterbuch nach und ergänzen Sie diese Listen mit weiteren Wortkombinationen.

work/worker collocations

(compound nouns)	work ______ (*Arbeitserlaubnis*)
	______ worker (*Arbeiter, der aus dem Ausland heimkehrt*)
(verbs)	______ work (*Arbeit finden*)
	______ work (*Arbeit suchen*)
(verb + prep)	look for ______ (*Arbeit suchen*)
(adj)	Polish ______ (*polnischer Arbeiter*)
(adj + prep)	willing to ______ (*arbeitswillig*)

______ / 16 Punkte

Sie können auch Wortkombinationen zu einem bestimmten Thema sammeln. Diese können Sie dann später zu Netzwerken zusammenfügen, wie z. B. zum Thema „Migrant workers".

Aufgabe 3

Match words from A and B to make phrases that describe what migrant workers "do". (The collocations are all in the text.)

	A		**B**
1	apply for	a	job benefits
2	seek	b	home
3	get	c	a new life
4	return	d	work
5	suffer	e	low wages
6	work for	f	work permits
7	build	g	social services
8	soak up	h	poverty

1	2	3	4	5	6	7	8

______ / 8 Punkte

Are rap artists responsible for the explosion of gang culture?

By **Ed Caesar**, 10 August, 2007

A Why are we asking this now?
A year-long study, which was commissioned by the UK Government, concluded yesterday that black teenagers urgently need new role models. The report called for a shift from 'rap stars, sports personalities and celebrities, to successful businessmen, lawyers and doctors'.

B Why pick on rap artists?
Since hip hop began in the poor, predominantly black neighbourhoods of New York in the 1970s, the genre has had an association with gang culture and violence. Lyrics often include references to drive-by shootings and drug-dealing. Rap and other urban genres are often the music choices of British gang members. Fatalities and injuries from gun and knife violence at hip-hop gigs have not helped the genre's image.

C Do rappers themselves promote a negative lifestyle?
Yes and no. Ever since the deaths of two prominent American rappers, Tupac Shakur and Biggie Smalls, in the mid-1990s, mainstream hip hop has become increasingly commercial. Rappers such as P Diddy, Jay-Z and 50 Cent have become multimillionaire businessmen with their own empires. These high-fliers argue that they promote an excellent lifestyle for teenagers – because, despite under-privileged upbringings, they have created successful business careers. Indeed, many in the top rank of hip hop are now pop stars with views on global 'issues'. It is no longer a surprise to see 50 Cent sitting next to Bono at a charity dinner to raise money for Africa.

D In Britain's urban scenes, however, the boundaries between music and behaviour are less straightforward. Metropolitan Police officers have found direct links between specific lyrics – particularly by British rap artists – and specific murders in the black community. Meanwhile, in America, a recent study by the Prevention Research Centre (Pire) concluded that, after assessing 1,000 students, rap music was consistently associated with alcohol use, illicit drug use, and aggressive behaviour.
Surely gang culture is fostered by more than just music?

E John Pitts, who is the professor of socio-legal studies at the University of Bedfordshire, recently conducted research into gang members in south London, and concluded that many teenagers were 'reluctant gangsters'. "These young people are stuck on their estates," he said in *The Guardian*, yesterday. "They can't get out because the waiting lists for social housing are so long there is nowhere for them to go. When young people resist gang involvement, they or their families can be attacked. In south London, 75 per cent of gangs involved kids who were not in school and were working as runners for drugs gangs. This is when their aspirations start to become unconventional, success for them is moving up the ladder within that gang until they take over and run their own young people."

F Hattie Collins, editor of the UK Urban magazine *RWD*, says that "music does play a small part, and it's something we need to look at, but so does the internet and film. There is a constant barrage of influences that kids are exposed to, or are exposing themselves to. I can't see a direct link between rap artists and violence. Young urban kids – and by the way, that means white, Asian, and black kids – could behave in the way they are behaving without the music."

538 words

Lesen Sie den Text und bearbeiten Sie die Aufgaben. Machen Sie sich keine Sorgen, wenn Sie nicht gleich alles verstehen; Sie werden sich ausführlich mit diesem Text in → STEP 6 beschäftigen.

adapted from: **The Independent**, 10 August, 2007

Aufgabe 1

Complete this index card. Only use your dictionary if you have to.

use

verb	noun (person)	noun (abstract)	adjective
use	______	______ *Gebrauch*	______ *brauchbar*
		______ *Verwendung*	______ *gebraucht*
		______ *Missbrauch*	______ *nützlich*
		______ *Missbrauch*	______ *nutzlos*

idiom: ______ *es hat keinen Sinn (etwas zu tun)*

structures: ______ *Ich bin es gewohnt, Tennis zu spielen.*

______ *Früher spielte ich Tennis.*

____ / 12 Punkte

Aufgabe 2

Complete the sentences using a suitable form of the word in brackets.

A recent report has called for new role models for black teenagers, showing people who have ______[1] (succeed) lifestyles such as lawyers and doctors. Gang ______[2] (violent) is often associated with rap ______[3] (musician) and its lyrics often refer to ______[4] (shoot) and other ______[5] (fatal). Some experts ______[6] (belief), however, that hip hop is not ______[7] (responsibility) for ______[8] (aggression) behaviour: the ______[9] (wait) list for ______[10] (society) housing is so long that there is nowhere else for ______[11] (youth) urban kids to go. Other experts claim that ______[12] (influence) such as film and the internet are a part of the ______[13] (cause) of the kids' ______[14] (behave).

____ / 14 Punkte

Aufgabe 3

Which word on the right (a, b, c or d) does not collocate with the word on the left? Replace the wrong word with your own word which fits the series.

1	**rap**	a star	b music	c lyric	d behaviour	
2	**black**	a teenager	b career	c community	d neighbourhood	
3	**drug**	a housing	b gang	c crime	d violence	
4	**gang**	a member	b violence	c gig	d involvement	
5	**urban**	a genre	b drug	c scene	d kids	

____ / 5 Punkte

Aufgabe 4

Find phrases in the text with the same meaning as the words in brackets. The letter for the paragraph where you can find the answer will help.

1 Rap artists claim that they (show young people how to live properly)
____. (paragraph C)

2 Many urban kids have (a poor childhood) ____________________
____. (paragraph C)

3 Rap music is associated with aggressive behaviour and (illegal drug-taking)
____. (paragraph D)

4 Young people on housing estates find it hard to (refuse to become part of a gang)
____. (paragraph E)

5 Once they join, gang members are only interested in (getting to the top)
____. (paragraph E)

____ / 5 Punkte

Aufgabe 5

Use words from the text and other collocations that you know or find in your dictionary to make a word web.

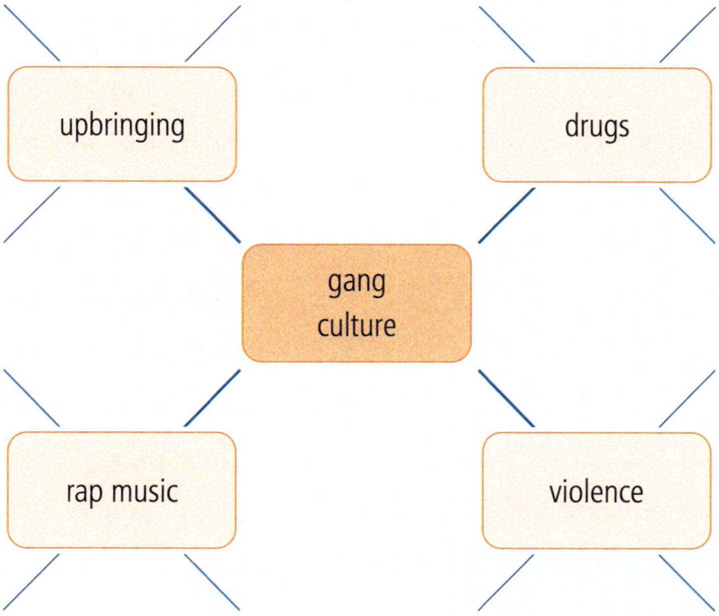

freie Aufgabe

Ich habe ____ Minuten für diesen Abschnitt gebraucht.

Ich habe ____ Mal ein Wörterbuch verwendet.

Ich habe ____ von 72 Punkten.

Jetzt kontrollieren Sie alle Antworten im Lösungsheft auf den Seiten 6–8.

STEP 6

Mediation Skills 1: Giving the gist in German
Topics: The world of work, Migrant workers; Youth culture, Music

Bei den Mediationsaufgaben (Englisch–Deutsch) wird eine von zwei wesentlichen Fähigkeiten verlangt:
1) Eine Redewendung / ein Satz aus dem Text ist sinngemäß ins Deutsche zu übertragen oder zu erklären (**giving the gist of the text**);
2) Fragen zum Text sind auf Deutsch zu beantworten oder eine Aussage ist auf Deutsch zusammenzufassen.
In diesem STEP befassen wir uns mit Punkt 1 (oben); in → STEP 7 werden wir uns mit Punkt 2 befassen.

Giving the gist of the text

Bei dieser Art von Mediationsaufgabe sollen Sie die wesentliche Aussage einer Textstelle in Ihren eigenen Worten so wiedergeben, dass jemand, der kein Englisch spricht, sie auch versteht. Es wird keine wortwörtliche Übersetzung verlangt.

- **Aufgabe lesen:** Die Aufgabe ist zwar auf Deutsch, aber Sie sollten sie trotzdem sorgfältig lesen.
- **Textstelle suchen:** Suchen Sie die relevante Textstelle und markieren Sie sie.
- **Zusammenhang überprüfen:** Lesen Sie die vorangegangenen und nachfolgenden Sätze bzw. Absätze, um sicher zu gehen, dass Sie die Textstelle richtig verstanden haben. Es geht immer um den Zusammenhang im Text. (→ STEP 1)
- **Redewendung nachschlagen:** Bei einer Redewendung (*idiom*) können Sie im Wörterbuch nachschlagen, ob sie dort erklärt wird. Aber kontrollieren Sie, dass Sie die Erklärung verwenden, die zum Kontext des Textes passt. (→ STEP 4)
- **Textstelle zusammenfassen:** Schreiben Sie den Satz / die Redewendung in Ihren eigenen Worten. Sie dürfen die Textstelle nicht „Wort für Wort" wiedergeben. Sie können z. B. den Satz umschreiben, Passivsätze in Aktivsätze oder Nomen- in Verbkonstruktionen umwandeln.
- **Text überprüfen:** Kontrollieren Sie zum Schluss, ob Ihr Text richtiges und gutes Deutsch ist.

Um diese Fähigkeiten zu üben, schauen wir uns wieder den Text „Poles Apart" (→ STEP 5, Seite 18) an.

Aufgabe 1

Read the text "Poles Apart" and complete this summary with a word or words from the text. (Each line represents one word.)

In 2004 Britain opened its ____ ____[1] to the new member states of the European Union and was taken by surprise by a flood of ____ ____[2]. Nearly 800,000 Eastern Europeans applied for ____ ____[3] in a huge ____ ____[4]. Now though many Poles are returning home because they can't find work any more in the UK. Other ____ ____[5] are also persuading them to go home: ____[6] in Poland are rising faster than in the UK and the ____ ____[7] there has dropped from 14% to 10%. The Polish ____[8] is growing at over 6%, while many migrant workers only find ____[9] work in Britain. It now seems that they think they will find better ____ ____[10] at home.

____ / 10 Punkte

Aufgabe 2

Für die Bedeutung zählt nur die Verwendung des Wortes oder der Wörter im Kontext!

Choose the correct meaning of these words as used in the text "Poles Apart".

1 flood (line 5)
  a a large amount of water covering an area that is usually dry
  b a very large number of things or people that appear at the same time

2 cheap (line 5)
  a costing little money or less money than you expected
  b low in price and quality

3 wave (line 6)
  a a sudden increase in a particular activity or feeling
  b a large number of people or things suddenly moving or appearing somewhere

4 soar (line 17)
  a to rise very quickly (value, amount, level)
  b to rise quickly and smoothly up into the air

5 benefit (line 19)
  a an advantage that something gives you
  b money provided by the government to people who need financial help

6 consideration (line 37)
  a the act of thinking carefully about something
  b things that must be thought about when you are planning or deciding something

7 trigger (line 45)
  a to make something happen suddenly
  b to cause a device to start functioning

8 stir (line 48)
  a (of a feeling or a mood) to begin to be felt
  b to try to cause trouble

9 speculation (line 48)
  a the act of forming opinions about what has happened or what might happen without knowing all the facts
  b the activity of buying and selling goods or shares in a company in the hope of making a profit, but with the risk of losing money

10 mount (line 64)
  a to organize and begin something
  b to increase gradually

1	2	3	4	5
6	7	8	9	10

_____ / 10 Punkte

Aufgabe 3

Which phrases/sentences in the text match these German paraphrases.

Bei Mediationsaufgaben geht es immer um den Sinn und nicht um eine wortwörtliche Übersetzung.

1 Polnische Migranten haben den britischen Arbeitsmarkt mit billigen Arbeitskräften überschwemmt.

____

2 Sie haben wirtschaftliche Starthilfe gesucht.

____

3 Der Zustrom der Polen hat Schauergeschichten in der Boulevardpresse ausgelöst.

____

4 Jetzt, wo sie weg sind, fängt man an, sich den Kopf über einen Mangel an Arbeitskräften zu zerbrechen.

____

5 Als Folge des wirtschaftlichen Abschwungs in Großbritannien werden wir in nächster Zeit mehr Polen sehen, die dorthin zurückzukehren, wo es gute Jobangebote gibt.

____

____

_____ / 5 Punkte

Es gibt immer mehr als eine Möglichkeit, den Sinn eines Satzes ins Deutsche zu übertragen. Man kann Satzumstellungen und andere Stilmittel – z. B. die Ersetzung von Nomen durch Verben – verwenden, um einem Satz seinen eigenen Stil zu verleihen.

Aufgabe 4

Complete the summaries of these sentences from the text, using the words in brackets.

1 The immigration wave took Britain by surprise. (lines 6–7)

(*überrascht*) Die Flut an ____

____.

(*nicht vorbereitet; Überschwemmung*) Großbritannien war ______________________

____.

2 Financial considerations are now driving them home again. (lines 37–38)

(*Überlegungen*) Wirtschaftliche ______________________________________

____.

(*überlegen; wirtschaftlich sinnvoll*) Sie ______________________________

____.

3 Builders are particularly in demand as the country pours money into infrastructure. (lines 58–60)

(*gefragt; investieren*) Bauarbeiter ______________________________________

____.

(*hoch im Kurs; ausgeben*) Weil das Land viel Geld ______________________

____.

Bei der Mediationsaufgabe geht es darum, die Inhalte vollständig wiederzugeben. Kontrollieren Sie immer, dass Sie alle Informationen im Satz berücksichtigt haben.

4 Polish employers have trekked out to London job fairs looking for labour. (lines 61–63)

(*London; reisen; suchen*) Polnische Arbeitgeber ______________________________

____.

(*Londoner; pilgern*) Auf der Suche ______________________________________

____.

______ / 8 Punkte

Schwierig wird es, wenn man einen Satz oder eine Redewendung im Kontext des Textes erklären soll. Versuchen Sie nun, Aufgabe 5 zu lösen.

Aufgabe 5

Geben Sie den Sinn dieser Überschrift aus der *Times* in Ihren eigenen Worten wieder:

(lines 49–50)

GET YOUR TAPS FIXED WHILE YOU CAN

Die Zeitung hat diese Überschrift gewählt, um deutlich zu machen, dass

____

____

____

______ / 2 Punkte

Aufgabe 1

Complete this crossword. The answers are all words from "Are rap artists responsible for the explosion of gang culture?"

Lesen Sie den Text „Are rap artists responsible for the explosion of gang culture?" (→ STEP 5, Seite 21) noch einmal und bearbeiten Sie die Aufgaben.

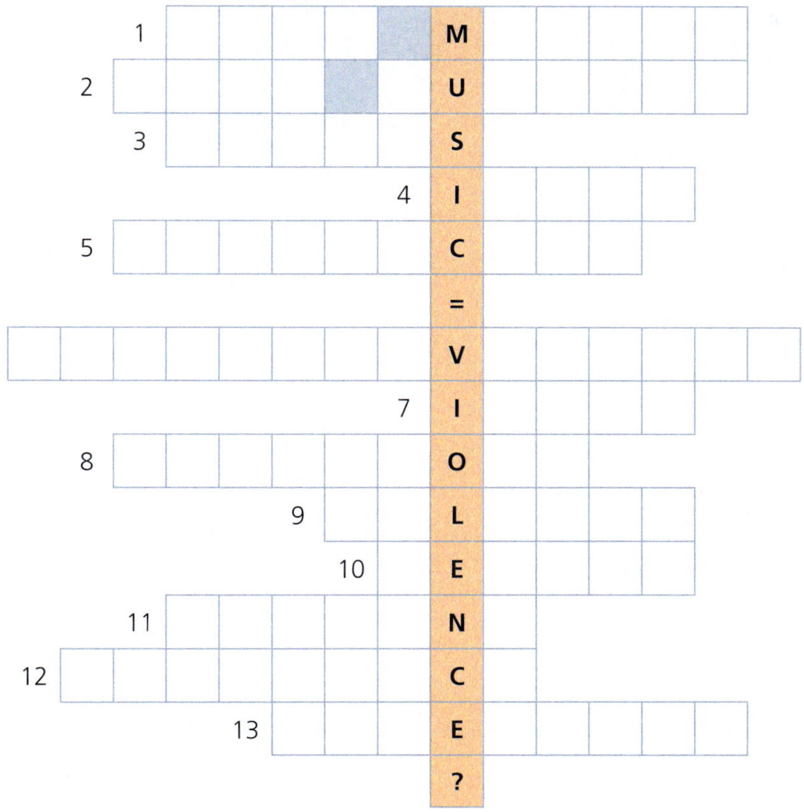

1 A report says that young blacks need new ...
2 Rap music has been associated with ... since it began in New York in the 1970s.
3 The words of a song.
4 The impression that a person, or a thing, gives to the public.
5 An adjective meaning "to do with trade or business".
6 If you are very poor as a child you might have an ... upbringing.
7 An important subject or topic that people argue about or discuss.
8 The noun form of "behave".
9 A synonym for "illegal".
10 Young people in parts of London find it hard to ... joining a gang.
11 Places to live that are provided by the state are called "social ...".
12 Not only music, but also the internet and films have a big ... on kids.
13 Successful rap musicians say that they promote a positive ... for young blacks.

_____ / 13 Punkte

Aufgabe 2

Which phrases/sentences in the text match these German paraphrases?

1 Gangmitglieder bevorzugen Musikrichtungen mit Großstadtfeeling.

____

____

2 Der Ruf der Hip-Hop-Musik leidet durch Gewaltexzesse bei den Konzerten.

____

____

3 Rap-Stars sind gern gesehene Gäste auf Wohltätigkeitsveranstaltungen.

____

____

4 Jugendliche sind Dauerkonsumenten von medialen Einflüssen, ob sie es wollen oder nicht.

____

____

5 Großstadtjugendliche aller Rassen könnten sich auch ohne den Einfluss der Musik so verhalten, wie sie sich verhalten.

____

____

_____ / 5 Punkte

Aufgabe 3

Complete these paraphrases of sentences from the text. The words in the box will help you.

Aufstieg • Anführer • britisch • Drogenmissbrauch • erfolgreich • Ergebnis • Gewalt • Hand in Hand • hinter • Laufbursche • stecken • trennen • Untersuchungen

1 In Britain's urban scenes, however, the boundaries between music and violent behaviour are less straightforward.

In ______________________ Städten aber kann man Musik und

______________________ nicht so einfach ______________________.

2 Surely gang culture is fostered by more than just music?

Aber ______________________ nicht mehr ______________________ den Gangs als nur Musik?

3 Success for them is moving up the ladder within that gang until they take over and run their own young people.

Eine ______________________ Karriere bedeutet für sie den

______________________ innerhalb der Gang, bis sie zu

______________________ mit eigenen ______________________ werden.

4 In America a recent study concluded that rap music was consistently associated with alcohol use, illicit drug use, and aggressive behaviour.

______________________ in den USA kamen zu dem ______________________,

dass Rap immer ______________________ mit Alkohol- und

______________________ und Aggression geht.

_____ / 13 Punkte

Aufgabe 4

Use the tips in the bubbles to write a summary in German of the following two sentences. The words in the box will help you.

Use *"seit"* + *Nomen*.

These words are not so important for the general meaning and can be left out.

Use one word meaning "poor neighbourhood".

1 Since hip hop began in the poor, predominantly black neighbourhoods of New York in the 1970s, the genre has had an association with gang culture and violence.

Use an adjective.

You can now use "hip hop" instead of "genre".

Use *"man"* + *Verb*.

Gang • gewalttätig • Ghetto • in Verbindung bringen • schwarz • Ursprung

Seit seinem ____

____

____

_____ / 6 Punkte

What sort of people are these "high-fliers"?

Don't use "argumentieren"!

Can you say this in two words?

2 These high-fliers argue that they promote an excellent lifestyle for teenagers – because, despite underprivileged upbringings, they have created successful business careers.

Can you say this in one word?

Use a noun instead of the adjective.

What sort of "teenagers"?

Benachteiligung • ehrgeizige Rap-Künstler • einen Standpunkt vertreten • Erfolge im Geschäftsleben vorweisen können • schwarze Jugendliche • Vorbildwirkung haben

_____ / 6 Punkte

Aufgabe 5

Ergänzen Sie die Sätze 1 und 2 um jeweils zwei der Punkte a–d und geben Sie den Inhalt in Ihren eigenen Worten wieder (keine wortwörtliche Übersetzung).

Bei der Mediation müssen Sie sicher gehen, dass Sie alle wichtigen Informationen wiedergeben, auch die, die nur aus dem Kontext des Textes zu erschließen sind. In dieser Übung finden Sie die passenden Bedeutungen in den Sätzen a–d.

1 Indeed, many in the top rank of hip hop are now pop stars with views on global 'issues'. (lines 35–37)

a Their records are always at the top of the charts.
b They sing about environmental pollution.
c People copy their lifestyle.
d They are successful international artists.

Viele _____

2 John Pitts [...] concluded that many teenagers were "reluctant gangsters". (lines 56–61)

a They only like listening to rap music.
b They can't find anywhere else to live.
c The gangsters threaten them and their families.
d They see gangs as a way to success.

Ein Professor ist zu dem Schluss gekommen, dass _____

_____ / 6 Punkte

Ich habe _____ Minuten für diesen Abschnitt gebraucht.

Ich habe _____ Mal ein Wörterbuch verwendet.

Ich habe _____ von 84 Punkten.

Jetzt kontrollieren Sie alle Antworten im Lösungsheft auf den Seiten 8/9.

STEP 7

Mediation Skills 2: Answering questions in German
Topics: Media, Technology, Business

In diesem STEP geht es darum, Fragen zum Text auf Deutsch zu beantworten oder eine Aussage im Text in eigenen Worten auf Deutsch zusammenzufassen (vgl. → STEP 6).

Answering questions in German

Jetzt werden Sie alle Fähigkeiten brauchen, die Sie in den vorangegangenen STEPS geübt haben:

- den allgemeinen **Sinn** des Textes verstehen (→ STEP 1)
- unbekannte Wörter aus dem **Kontext** erkennen (→ STEP 2)
- Informationen aus dem Text **filtern** (→ STEP 3)
- unbekannte Wörter gegebenenfalls im **Wörterbuch** nachschlagen (→ STEP 4)
- Informationen **in eigenen Worten** auf Deutsch wiedergeben (→ STEP 6)
- Text **überprüfen**: Kontrollieren Sie zum Schluss, ob Ihr Text richtiges und gutes Deutsch ist.

Lesen Sie jetzt den Text, und bearbeiten Sie die Aufgaben.

What carriers aren't eager to tell you about texting

A TEXT messaging is a wonderful business to be in: about 2.5 trillion messages were sent from cellphones worldwide in 2008. The public assumes that the carriers' costs are far higher than they actually are, and profit margins are concealed by a heavy curtain.

B Democrat Senator Herb Kohl, of Wisconsin, dared to look behind the curtain. He wanted to know why all four of the major American carriers decided during the last three years to increase the pay-per-use price for text messages from 10 cents to 20 cents. The decision could not have come from a dearth of business: the number of messages sent in 2008 was up 32% from 2007. Experts estimate 3.3 trillion messages will be sent in 2009.

C T-Mobile and AT&T argued in their replies to Mr Kohl that the pay-per-use price of a text message is relatively unimportant because most messaging is done as part of an unlimited package. With a $10 or $15 monthly fee for text messaging, customers of T-Mobile, AT&T and Sprint can effectively bring the price per message down to a penny, if they fully use their monthly allowance.

D A text message initially travels as a radio signal from a cellphone to the closest base-station tower and is then transferred to the digital cables of the telephone network; near its destination it is converted back into a radio signal for the final leg, from base-station to cellphone. In the cable portion of its journey, a file of such infinitesimal size is inconsequential. Srinivasan Keshav, a professor of computer science at the University of Waterloo, in Ontario, said: "Text messages are small. Even though a trillion seems like a lot to carry, it isn't."

E Perhaps the costs for the radio signal at either end are high – the spectrum of radio waves is not endless, after all, and carriers pay dearly for the rights to use it. But text messages are not just tiny; they are also free riders, inserted into what's called a control channel – the space reserved for the operation of the wireless network. That's why a text message is generally limited to 160 characters: it must not exceed the length of the message used for internal communication between tower and cellphone to set up a call. The channel uses the same space whether a text message is inserted or not.

F According to Professor Keshav, once a carrier invests in the centralized storage equipment – storing a terabyte now costs only $100 and is dropping – and the staff to maintain it, its costs are basically covered. "Operating costs are relatively insensitive to volume," he said. "It doesn't cost the carrier much more to transmit a hundred million messages than a million."

terabyte: 1,024 gigabytes or 1012 bytes. The prefix "tera" comes from the Greek word meaning "monster."

CROSSING OVER

Arbeitsbuch zum Übergang in die Fachoberschule

Answer Key

Cornelsen

ANSWER **KEY**

STEP 1

Aufgabe 1
1 somewhere
2 something
3 something
4 Somehow
5 Somebody
6 something
7 something

Aufgabe 2
c A woman knew how to save a man's life because she saw what to do in a hospital series on television.

Aufgabe 3
1 photographic shop
2 had a diabetic fit / collapsed
3 resuscitated
4 heart massage
5 remembered the techniques
6 paramedic
7 saved his life
8 unbelievable

PRACTICE 1

Aufgabe 1
A 6
B 4
C 1
D 5
E 2
F 3

Aufgabe 2
1 is a first sentence and 4 is a last sentence. They are from text F.
2 is a first sentence and 6 is a last sentence. They are from text C.
3 is a first sentence and 5 is a last sentence. They are from text E.

Aufgabe 3
A 2
B 1
C 4
D 6
E 5
F 3

Aufgabe 4
A 5 *(film-makers, visual effects)*
B 6 *(parental, car)*
C 1 *(gamers, body mass index, overweight)*
D 2 *(drivers, mobile phones)*
E 4 *(employers, authorities, websites)*
F 3 *(player, loner)*

Aufgabe 5
1 new
2 digital
3 real
4 extremely
5 specially
6 extraordinary
7 digitally
8 Amazingly
9 incredible
10 actually
11 unbelievable
12 completely
13 entirely
14 physical

STEP 2

Aufgabe 1
1 diabetes *(line 13)*
2 collapse *(line 4)*
3 pulse *(line 25)*
4 heart massage *(line 8)*
5 effectively *(line 6)*
6 c
7 e
8 d
9 a
10 b

Aufgabe 2
1 diabetic *(line 3)*
2 resuscitate *(line 7)*
3 restart *(line 33)*
4 reunite *(line 37)*
5 unbelievable *(line 47)*

Aufgabe 3
1 fairly *(line 32)*
2 really *(line 36)*
3 actually *(line 45)*
4 obvious *(line 48)*

Aufgabe 4
1 b 2 c 3 a 4 c 5 d

PRACTICE 2

Aufgabe 1

Words in the text		International words/similar German words	Other German words
1	data	Daten	Informationen
2	computer	Computer	Rechner
3	manipulate	manipulieren	bearbeiten
4	image	Image	Bild
5	film-maker	Filmemacher	Regisseur/in
6	create	kreieren	schaffen
7	action	Action	Handlung
8	sequence	Sequenz	Szene
9	fan	Fan	Anhänger/in
10	feeling	Feeling	Gefühl

Aufgabe 2

Adjectives formed from *nouns*		
-al	*-y*	*-ful*
educational	angry	powerful
industrial	healthy	successful
Adjectives formed from *verbs*		
-ive	*-able*	
creative	advisable	
progressive	changeable	
supportive	manageable	

Aufgabe 3

Nouns formed from *verbs*		Nouns formed from *adjectives*	
-(a)tion	*-ment*	*-ity*	*-ness*
creation	agreement	creativity	fairness
education	employment	productivity	happiness
imagination	management	stupidity	illness

Aufgabe 4

1 incredible
2 unlikely
3 improbable
4 impossible
5 unpleasant
6 impolite
7 unpopular
8 unsuccessful
9 irresponsible
10 disagreeable
11 dishonest
12 illegal

STEP 3

Aufgabe 1

1 B
2 A
3 D
4 C

Aufgabe 2

1 b 2 a 3 c 4 a 5 d

Aufgabe 3

1 Zusammengehörigkeit
2 Verbundenheit
3 Geräte
4 Geschwister

PRACTICE 3

Aufgabe 1

A 2
B 8
C 6
D 1
E 4
F 5

Aufgabe 2

1 99% of boys and 94% of girls aged 12–17
2 *Guitar Hero*
3 Solving problems or playing a sport
4 Talk on the phone, email or spend time with a friend
5 Decide how a community should be run
6 To teach young people about social issues/ problems

Aufgabe 3

1 report/study/survey
2 gaming
3 pastime
4 excessive
5 addiction
6 violence
7 online
8 issues
9 educational
10 confront
11 virtual
12 parents
13 attention

STEP 4

Aufgabe 1

Which question from the Skill box can I answer with yes?		**Comments**	**Word class (Wortart)**	**Definition**	**German**
pedal	Nr. 2	*Pedal* (German noun)	verb	to turn or press the pedals on a bicycle	in die Pedale treten / Rad fahren
traffic	5	–	noun	vehicles on a road at a certain time	Verkehr
nonsense	3	*Nonsens*	noun	ideas, statements or beliefs that you think are untrue	Unsinn
menace	–	–	noun	sth that may cause damage or be dangerous	Gefahr
pedestrian	5	*use iPods, not in trucks, not on motorbikes, etc*	noun	person travelling on foot	Fußgänger/in
proliferation	–	–	noun	sudden increase in the number / amount of sth.	Vermehrung/ Ausbreitung
inadvertently	6	–	adverb	by accident	versehentlich
brake	4 + 5	*brake (n); see swerve*	verb	to make sth. slow down	bremsen
swerve	5	*sth you do on a bike to avoid an accident*	verb	to turn suddenly	ausscheren
nasty	5 (6)	*sth to do with an accident*	adjective	very bad/ unpleasant	schlimm/ unangenehm

Aufgabe 2

1 threat
2 a sense / an air / a hint of menace
3 threaten
4 menacing, menacingly
5 noun and verb
6 heavy / rush-hour / local / through traffic; in traffic; traffic congestion / police; commuter / freight / passenger traffic

PRACTICE 4

Aufgabe 1

1 Meaning 1: Worry and anxiety that you show by behaving in a nervous way
2 uncountable
3 forgetful
4 absent-mindedly, absent-mindedness
5 nonchalance
6 He was leaning casually against the wall
7 The bike came hurtling towards them

Aufgabe 2

1 in a daze
2 mobile
3 stationery; Schreibwaren/Briefpapier
4 proportionate
5 noun: dissatisfaction;
verbs: displease, disprove;
adjectives: disreputable, dissatisfied

Aufgabe 3

1 noun; Bewegung
2 a eine gute Tat
b der Reihenfolge nach
c die Jahrhundertwende
d eine Drehung der Schraube

Aufgabe 4

2 up
3 about
4 up
5 out
6 for
7 up
8 forward to
9 out
10 up
11 up with
12 on with
13 out
14 off
15 on
16 to
17 off
18 on
19 off
20 around
21 up

STEP 5

Aufgabe 1

employ

verb	noun (person)	noun (abstract)	adjective
employ	employer	employment	employed
	employee		employable

opposites: unemployment; unemployed; unemployable

collocation: employment agency

synonyms: employee = worker, labourer (BE), laborer (AE)

verb	noun (person)	noun (abstract)	adjective
Work	worker	work	working/workable
labour	labourer	labour	

Aufgabe 2

job collocations		
(compound nouns)	(verb)	seek a job *(Arbeit suchen)*
job market *(Arbeitsmarkt)*	(verb + prep)	look for a job *(Arbeit suchen)*
job benefit *(Arbeitslosengeld)*		
job offer *(Jobangebot)*	(adj)	full-time job *(Vollzeitjob)*
job fair *(Jobmesse)*	(adj)	part-time job *(Teilzeitjob)*
job opportunity *(Arbeitsmöglichkeit)*	(adj + prep)	eager for a job *(arbeitswillig)*

work/worker collocations

(compound nouns)	work permit (*Arbeitserlaubnis*)
	returnee worker (*Arbeiter, der aus dem Ausland heimkehrt*)
(verbs)	find work (*Arbeit finden*)
	seek work (*Arbeit suchen*)
(verb + prep)	look for work / a job (*Arbeit suchen*)
(adj)	Polish worker (*polnischer Arbeiter*)
(adj + prep)	willing to work (*arbeitswillig*)

Aufgabe 3

1 f 2 d 3 a 4 b 5 h 6 e 7 c 8 g

PRACTICE 5

Aufgabe 1

use

verb	**noun (person)**	**noun (abstract)**	**adjective**
use	user	use = *Gebrauch*	usable = *brauchbar*
		usage = *Verwendung*	used = *gebraucht*
		abuse = *Missbrauch*	useful = *nützlich*
		misuse = *Missbrauch*	useless = *nutzlos*

idiom: It's no use (doing sth) = *es hat keinen Sinn (etwas zu tun)*

structures: I'm used to playing tennis. = *Ich bin es gewohnt, Tennis zu spielen.*

I used to play tennis. = *Früher spielte ich Tennis.*

Aufgabe 2

1 successful
2 violence
3 music
4 shootings
5 fatalities
6 believe
7 responsible
8 aggressive
9 waiting
10 social
11 young
12 influences
13 cause
14 behaviour

Aufgabe 3

1 d artist, song, concert
2 b artist, culture, singer
3 a culture, use, addict
4 c culture, fight, initiation
5 b gang, lifestyle

Aufgabe 4

1 promote an excellent lifestyle for teenagers
2 an under-privileged upbringing
3 illicit drug use
4 resist gang involvement
5 moving up the ladder

Aufgabe 5

Freie Aufgabe

STEP 6

Aufgabe 1

1 job market
2 cheap labour
3 work permits
4 immigration wave
5 financial considerations
6 wages
7 unemployment rate
8 economy
9 part-time
10 job opportunities

Aufgabe 2

1 b 2 a 3 b 4 a 5 b 6 b 7 a 8 a 9 a 10 a

Aufgabe 3

1 Poles have provided the British economy with a flood of cheap labour *(lines 4–6)*
2 They were coming to get a financial leg-up *(lines 35–36)*
3 The influx of Poles triggered tabloid scare stories (lines 44–45)
4 Now their departure has stirred doleful speculation about labour shortages *(lines 47–49)*
5 As the economy turns sour in Britain, you can expect many more Poles to head for where the job opportunities lie: home *(lines 72–75)*

Aufgabe 4

1 Die Flut an Immigranten hat Großbritannien überrascht.
Großbritannien war auf eine solche Überschwemmung durch Immigranten nicht vorbereitet.
2 Wirtschaftliche Überlegungen zwingen sie, nach Hause zurückzukehren.
Sie überlegen nun, ob es nicht wirtschaftlich sinnvoll wäre, nach Hause zurückzukehren.
3 Bauarbeiter sind besonders gefragt, da das Land viel Geld in die Infrastruktur investiert.
Weil das Land viel Geld für die Infrastruktur ausgibt, stehen Bauarbeiter besonders hoch im Kurs.
4 Polnische Arbeitgeber sind nach London gereist, um Arbeitskräfte bei den Jobbörsen zu suchen.
Auf der Suche nach Arbeitskräften sind polnische Arbeitgeber zu Londoner Jobmessen gepilgert.

Aufgabe 5

Die Zeitung hat diese Überschrift gewählt, um deutlich zu machen, dass die Zeiten der günstigen Arbeitskräfte/Handwerker aus Osteuropa bald vorbei sein werden.

PRACTICE 6

Aufgabe 1
1 role models
2 gang culture
3 lyrics
4 image
5 commercial
6 underprivileged
7 issue
8 behaviour
9 illicit
10 resist
11 housing
12 influence
13 lifestyle

Aufgabe 2
1 Rap and other urban genres are often the music choices of British gang members. *(lines 17–18)*
2 Fatalities and injuries from gun and knife violence at hip-hop gigs have not helped the genre's image. *(lines 19–21)*
3 It is no longer a surprise to see 50 Cent sitting next to Bono at a charity dinner to raise money for Africa. *(lines 37–40)*
4 There is a constant barrage of influences that kids are exposed to, or are exposing themselves to. *(lines 81–83)*
5 Young urban kids – and by the way, that means white, Asian, and black kids – could behave in the way they are behaving without the music. *(lines 85–88)*

Aufgabe 3
1 In **britischen** Städten aber kann man Musik und **Gewalt** nicht so einfach **trennen**.
2 Aber **steckt** nicht mehr **hinter** den Gangs als nur Musik?
3 Eine **erfolgreiche** Karriere bedeutet für sie den **Aufstieg** innerhalb der Gang, bis sie zu **Anführer** mit eigenen **Laufburschen** werden.
4 **Untersuchungen** in den USA kamen zu dem **Ergebnis**, dass Rap immer **Hand in Hand** mit Alkohol- und **Drogenmissbrauch** und Aggression geht.

Aufgabe 4
1 Seit seinem Ursprung in den 1970er Jahren in den schwarzen Ghettos New Yorks hat man Hip-Hop in Verbindung mit gewalttätigen Gangs gebracht.
2 Die ehrgeizigen Rap-Künstler vertreten den Standpunkt, dass sie Vorbildwirkung für schwarze Jugendliche haben, weil sie trotz Benachteiligung Erfolge im Geschäftsleben vorweisen können.

Aufgabe 5
Lösungsvorschläge
1 Viele erfolgreiche Hip-Hop-Künstler sind internationale Stars geworden und werden nach Ihrer Meinung zu wichtigen aktuellen Themen gefragt, die die ganze Welt beschäftigen.
2 Ein Professor ist zu dem Schluss gekommen, dass viele Jugendliche nur ungern Gangmitglieder sind, aber sie haben keine Möglichkeit, anderswo zu leben und die Gangs setzen sie und ihre Familien unter Druck.

STEP 7

Aufgabe 1
1 F: About 2.5 trillion text messages were sent worldwide in 2008. *(lines 2–4)*
2 T *(lines 4–6)*
3 T *(lines 6–7)*
4 F: The number of messages sent rose 32% in 2008 so a lack of business cannot have been the reason for price increases. *(lines 14–17)*
5 F: The cost of a pay-per-use text message doubled over the last three years. *(lines 10–14)*
6 T *(lines 23–24)*

Aufgabe 2
1 fee *(line 25)*
2 carriers *(line5)*
3 pay-per-use price *(line 13)*
4 unlimited package *(line 24)*
5 profit margin *(line 6)*
6 allowance *(line 29)*
7 dearth of business *(line 15)*

Aufgabe 3
1 – Man glaubt, Kosten müssen hoch sein
– Gewinnspanne wird geheim gehalten
2 Zahl der SMS um 32% gestiegen / das Geschäft boomt/floriert
3 Die meisten SMS sind in einem Flatrate-Tarif inbegriffen.

Aufgabe 4

1 radio *(line 39)*
2 tower *(line 32)*
3 cables *(line 33)*
4 network *(line 34)*
5 destination *(line 34)*
6 characters *(line 53)*
7 inserted *(line 49)*
8 channel *(line 50)*
9 reserved *(line 51)*
10 communication *(line 55)*
11 operating costs *(line 64)*
12 storage *(line 60)*
13 staff *(line 63)*
14 volume *(line 65)*

Aufgabe 5

1 - Radiosignal vom Absender/Handy zum Mobilfunkmast
  - digitales Festnetz
  - Radiosignal vom Mobilfunkmast zum (Ziel-) Handy
2 - 160 Zeichen
  - maximale Länge des Kontrollsignals/ Verbindungssignals
3 egal ob SMS auf Kontrollkanal eingefügt oder nicht
4 - Speicherkapazität
  - Mitarbeiter

Aufgabe 6

1 Die Mobilfunkunternehmen wollen nicht, dass die Öffentlichkeit darüber informiert wird, wie kostengünstig SMS geschickt werden können.
2 Die monatlichen Flatrate-Tarife sind eigentlich doch nicht so günstig, wie sie zunächst erscheinen.

Aufgabe 2

1 D
2 A
3 E
4 C
5 B

Aufgabe 3

1 - große neue Konsumentenschicht
  - viel Geld zum Ausgeben
  - sind noch jung / haben ein langes Leben vor sich
2 - sie kaufen ungern in Warenhäusern ein
  - sie lesen andere Zeitschriften als ihre Mütter
3 - Werbespots auf MTV / anderen jugendlichen Sendern
  - Internetwerbung auf Facebook
  - Vorstellung der Produkte für Studentinnen
  - niedrige Preisgestaltung
4 - parfümierte Hautpflegemittel
  - Werbung mit Supermodels/Schönheiten
  - überteuerte/teure Produkte
5 Alltagsprodukte / alte Hausmittel können genauso effektiv wie teure Kosmetika sein.

Aufgabe 4

1 Die ältere Generation / Generation der Babyboomers ist nicht mehr so wichtig, wie sie früher / im vorigen Jahrhundert war.
2 Sie wollen unbedingt ihre jugendliche Ausstrahlung beibehalten.
3 Die jungen Frauen sind für die Kosmetikfirmen nicht leicht zu erreichen.
4 Die Kosmetikfirmen versuchen, die junge Generation mit Argumenten/Informationen zu überzeugen, statt mit Schönheiten/ Supermodels.

PRACTICE 7

Aufgabe 1

Schönheit = *beauty*		**Industrie = *industry***	
cleanser cosmetics cream fragrance ingredient	lip gloss moisturizer puffiness scented skin care	advertising budget brand business campaign company consultant consumer	customer market marketing market research packaging product sales

STEP 8

Aufgabe 1
1 subject
2 foreground
3 background
4 In the top left-hand corner
5 In the top right-hand corner
6 in the bottom right-hand corner

Aufgabe 2
1 eye-catching feature
2 obviously (just)
3 Looking at the way
4 can assume
5 think
6 might be
7 probably
8 just (obviously)
9 wants to remind us
10 always

Aufgabe 3
1 label
2 caricature
3 symbol
4 speech bubble
5 sign
6 caption

Aufgabe 4
1 shows
2 has
3 is
4 says
5 is sitting
6 are
7 can
8 is looking
9 says
10 reads
11 call
12 is making
13 are
14 isn't
15 has
16 is
17 won't be

PRACTICE 8

Aufgabe 1
1 shows
2 is leaning
3 is holding
4 has
5 don't see
6 don't know
7 is
8 seems
9 is bending
10 looks
11 is helping
12 wants
13 has probably been
14 has drunk
15 feels
16 needs

Aufgabe 2
Main subject of photo:
woman sitting on ground

Where is she?
unknown town or city

How old is subject?
can't see – head on knees / dress and hairstyle for a young woman

Other people in photo?
alone

Time of photo?
unknown – seems to be dark

Other features in photo?
empty bottle next to hand, spilt liquid

Aim of photographer?
show effects of binge-drinking

Explanation of situation?
has been out with friends, had too much to drink, now feeling ill, friends have left her?

Aufgabe 3
Lösungsvorschlag
The photo shows a woman sitting on the ground somewhere in an unknown town or city. Her head is on her knees so that we cannot see how old she is but her dress and hairstyle suggest that she is a young woman. She is alone and it seems to be dark. There is a bottle lying next to her hand; some liquid has spilled out of the bottle.
I think the photographer wants to show the effects of binge-drinking. The woman has probably been out with friends and has drunk too much. Now she is feeling ill. Her friends seem to have left her sitting on her own. *(109 words)*

Aufgabe 4
1 This cartoon shows a typical boy's bedroom.
2 A boy is sitting at his computer.
3 Behind him, in the bottom right-hand corner, there is a football, but he is not interested in it.
4 In the background we can see the boy's mother.
5 She is standing in the doorway looking crossly at the boy.
6 In a speech bubble she says: "Nine hours in a row on the internet! Do you think that's good for your computer?"
7 Both the boy and the mother are overweight.
8 He is only interested in the internet and she is only worried about the expensive computer.
9 As a result, it is not surprising that the boy spends all his time inside.

Aufgabe 5
This cartoon shows a typical boy's bedroom. A boy is sitting at his computer. Behind him, in the bottom right-hand corner, there is a basketball, but he is not interested in it. In the background we can see the boy's mother. She is standing in the door-way looking crossly at the boy. In a speech bubble the boy says: "I'm not coming down for dinner, didn't you read my blog?"
The cartoonist is making the point that the internet doesn't always help people to communicate with each other. The boy is addicted to his weblog, but his mother probably doesn't know what a weblog is.

Aufgabe 6
Lösungsvorschlag
This cartoon shows a man visiting his son in prison. On the left we can see a young man in a prison cell. He looks unhappy. In the middle, a man is talking to him. In a speech bubble the man says: "I don't know where we went wrong with you son?!" Behind the man, on the right, there is another young man in a cell. He has a speech bubble that says: "… I'm over here, Dad."
I think the cartoonist is satirizing the fact that some parents don't really know their children very well. The father obviously hasn't spent much time with his son.

STEP 9

Aufgabe 1
1 y-axis
2 x-axis
3 line graph
4 segments
5 pie chart
6 table
7 bar chart

Aufgabe 2
1 violent crime in Britain
2 1981
3 2007
4 x-axis
5 y-axis
6 incidents
7 millions
8 two
9 1983
10 1991
11 1995
12 2001
13 2004
14 2006
15 2007

Aufgabe 3
1 Simple present
2 Simple past
3 b
4 c

Aufgabe 4

1 The figures **dropped slightly** from 1981 to 1983.
2/3 There was a **steady rise** in the figures from 1983 to 1991.
4/5 There was a **sharp increase** in the number of violent crimes up to 1995.
6 **Violent crime fell gradually** from 1995 to 2001.
7 Incidents of violent crime **climbed suddenly** from 2005 to 2006.
8 There was a **slow decrease** in the numbers from 2006 to 2007.

Aufgabe 5

Lösungsvorschlag

The two graphs show trends in the number of smokers, male and female respectively, in Japan, the UK and the USA. On the x-axis you can see the years from 1960 to 2000. The y-axis shows the percentage of adult male or female smokers. If we look at the trends in the number of adult male smokers, we can see from the left-hand graph that Japan had the highest number of male smokers from 1960 (80% of adult males) to 2000 (55%) and that the USA had the lowest number throughout (about 50% in 1960 to 25% in 2000). In every country, the number of adult male smokers declined steadily during this period, with the number of smokers in the UK and the USA halved by 2000. In contrast, Japan consistently had the lowest percentage of adult female smokers between 1960 and 2000 (staying around 14%). The UK had the highest percentage, peaking at about 45%, although this fell drastically from 1970 onwards to 25% in 2000. The USA mirrored the UK with a more gradual decline in numbers throughout this period. However, it is also important to note that the percentage ratio of male smokers to female in all countries is almost double, as the x-axis goes up to 90% on the graph representing male smoking trends, but only to 50% on the graph representing female smoking trends. *(229 words)*

PRACTICE 9

Aufgabe 1

This bar chart shows how many people use the internet in the world. The y-axis shows the geographic regions. The x-axis gives the number of users in millions. There are over 650 million internet users in Asia, followed by 390.1 million in Europe. North America and Latin America are the next two largest groups. According to the chart, there are only 54.2 million internet users in Africa and 45.9 million in the Middle East. The smallest group is Oceania/Australia with 20.6 million.

Aufgabe 2

Lösungsvorschlag

This pie chart shows the percentage of world internet users by geographic regions. The pie chart is divided into seven geographic regions. The largest percentage of internet users comes from Asia with 41.3%, followed by 24.8% in Europe. North America and Latin America are the next two largest groups. According to the chart, only 3.4% of internet users are from Africa and 2.9% come from the Middle East. The smallest group is Oceania/Australia with 1.3%.

Aufgabe 3

1 largest, not as high as
2 the smallest, highest, higher
3 the lowest, bigger than
4 not as big as
5 largest, smaller than

Aufgabe 4

1 There are more internet users in Europe than in North America.
2 There are fewer internet users in Latin America than in North America.
3 The most internet users are in Asia.
4 The least number of internet users come from Oceania/Australia.
5 Internet access in Oceania/Australia is about 10% more than in Europe.
6 Internet access in Europe is twice as high as in the Middle East.
7 Internet access in Latin America is about 20% less than in Europe.
8 Internet access in the Middle east is about the same as the world average.

Aufgabe 5
Lösungvorschlag

1 Oceania/Australia has the smallest number of internet users with only 1.3% of the total. However, internet access in Oceania/Australia is the second highest of all the geographic regions at 59.9%. The population of Oceania/Australia is not that large and is relatively wealthy, so it is probably quite easy for people to get internet access.
2 Africa has the lowest internet access rate of all the geographic regions at 5.6%. Only 3.4% of all the internet users in the world are from Africa. Africa has a very large population but it is not economically developed, so it is not easy for people to get internet access.
3 North America has only the third highest number of world internet users at 15.7% of the total. However, 73.1% of the population have access to the internet, which is the highest number for all the geographic regions. The population in America is not as big as in other regions, but it is economically very well developed, so it is easy for nearly everyone to get access to the internet.

STEP 10

Aufgabe 1
1 opinion composition, for and against composition
2 opinion composition
3 opinion composition
4 opinion composition
5 opinion composition, for and against composition
6 for and against composition
7 opinion composition

Aufgabe 2
Reality TV shows that humiliate their candidates should be banned.
Discuss this idea in about 200 words.

For and against composition

Introduction
some shows humiliate candidates, should they be banned?

Main part 1 – For
no information value, pure entertainment
degrading for candidates, do unpleasant tasks
viewing figures important, producers looking for new 'thrills'

Main part 2 – Against
candidates don't have to go on the show, want to be on show
freedom of choice for viewer, no one has to watch
form of censorship, who decides what is good/bad TV?

Conclusion
viewers decide what is shown on TV, people soon get bored

Aufgabe 3
1 C
2 A
3 D
4 B

Aufgabe 4
1 I personally believe that
2 The first thing to point out is that
3 although
4 The reason for this is that
5 We must also take into account that
6 therefore
7 The last point I'd like to make is that
8 Take for example
9 To sum up
10 I have no doubt that

This is an opinion composition.

PRACTICE 10

Aufgabe 1
1 Everyone knows that
2 There's no doubt in my mind that / I have no doubt that
3 although
4 Firstly
5 they claim
6 What's more
7 in particular
8 Another argument
9 such as
10 In spite of all this
11 And we must not forget
12 Finally
13 To sum up
14 I'm convinced that

Aufgabe 2

For

- stars have right to privacy - photographers wouldn't like it
- families affected - children suffer in particular
- exposed to dangers - e. g. kidnapping, black-mail, stalking

Against

- of interest to public - chance to see how they live
- most stars no problems - accept as part of job
- enough want publicity - keep careers going

Conclusion

- stars happy - so long as not in danger

Aufgabe 3

1 Every time there is a major sporting event, such as the Olympic Games or the Tour de France, there are always stories about doping in the news.

2 There is no doubt in my mind that sports stars who use steroids should be banned, but I'm not so sure that they should be banned for life.

3 The athletes that are caught by drugs test usually say that it is the pressure to win that forces them to use steroids, particularly if they are trying to come back after an injury.

4 Furthermore, they argue that if they don't take performance-enhancing drugs they will have no chance to compete at the highest level.

5 This argument is simply nonsense: just think of the damage they are doing to their own bodies, as well as the bad example they are setting for young people who want to start a career in sports.

6 What is more, they are cheating their fellow competitors, and if they win the financial gains they make are nothing more than fraud.

7 Last but not least, they are cheating all the spectators and fans who support them, which ruins the appeal of the sport for the future.

8 Taking everything into account, no one can seriously doubt that athletes who dope deserve to be banned.

9 In my opinion they should be banned for two years, after which they should be given a second chance.

Aufgabe 4

Lösungsvorschlag

Everyone has sat next to someone in a bus or train who talked loudly into their mobile phone for the whole journey. This is very annoying behaviour, but do we really need to ban mobiles completely?

Those who support this suggestion say that the use of mobile phones in public is a nuisance. They say that it is impossible to read, think or talk to a fellow passenger while someone else is talking loudly on the phone. In addition, they believe that the use of mobile phones adds to all the other noise of modern life, such as traffic, loud music and road-works, and that the noise is a health hazard. Furthermore, they claim that it is bad manners to use a mobile in public and that people should respect the privacy of other passengers.

On the other hand, we must not forget that mobile phones are an important part of our life and we need them to make appointments or to keep in contact with our friends. We must also take into account that there are already so many aspects of our lives that are controlled, such as smoking in public places, that we do not need any more laws. The most important problem, however, is that it would be impractical to enforce a ban. Thousands of passengers would become criminals for using their mobile phones.

All in all, I am of the opinion that the use of mobile phones in public places should be kept to a mini-mum, but this will only be possible if people learn to respect the privacy of their fellow travellers.

G Once one understands that a text message travels as a stowaway within a control channel, one sees the carriers' pricing plans in an entirely new light. The most profitable plan for the carriers will be the one that collects the most revenue from the customer: unlimited messaging, for which AT&T and Sprint charge $20 a month and T-Mobile, $15.

H Customers with unlimited monthly plans, like diners bringing a healthy appetite to an all-you-can-eat cafeteria, might think they're getting the best out of the arrangement. But the carriers, unlike the cafeteria owners, can provide unlimited quantities of "food" at virtually no cost to themselves – so long as it is served in bite-sized portions. 559 words

adapted from: **New York Times**, 28 December, 2008

Aufgabe 1

Are these statements about paragraphs A–C true or false?

Schauen Sie sich zunächst die Absätze A–C genauer an und bearbeiten Sie die Aufgaben 1–3.

		T	F
1	2.5 trillion text messages were sent in the USA in 2008.	☐	☐
2	People think that transporting text messages must be expensive.	☐	☐
3	People don't really know how much profit companies earn from text messaging.	☐	☐
4	The companies put their prices up because people were sending fewer text messages.	☐	☐
5	The cost of a pay-per-use text message rose by 32% from 2006 to 2007.	☐	☐
6	Most text messages are paid for as part of a monthly package.	☐	☐

_____ / 6 Punkte

Aufgabe 2

Match the highlighted words/phrases in paragraphs A–C to these German words.

1 Tarif ______________________

2 Mobilfunkunternehmen ______________________

3 Stückpreis ______________________

4 Flatrate ______________________

5 Gewinnspanne ______________________

6 Freibetrag ______________________

7 Kundenmangel ______________________

_____ / 7 Punkte

Aufgabe 3

Beantworten Sie folgende Aufgaben zu den Absätzen A–C auf Deutsch.

1 Warum sind SMS ein gewinnbringendes Geschäft für die Mobilfunkunternehmen? (*2 Punkte*)

– ______________________

– ______________________

2 Warum glaubte Senator Kohl, dass die Preiserhöhungen nicht gerechtfertigt waren?

____

3 Wieso behaupten die Mobilfunkunternehmen, dass der Stückpreis für SMS unwichtig sei?

____

_____ / 4 Punkte

Jetzt schauen Sie sich die Absätze D–F genauer an und bearbeiten Sie die Aufgaben 4 und 5.

Aufgabe 4

Complete the following summary of paragraphs D–F with words from the text.

Text messages are sent as ____________ 1 (*Funk-*) signals from the sender's mobile phone to the nearest base-station ____________ 2 (*Mobilfunkmast*); the messages are transferred through the digital ____________ 3 (*Kabel*) of the telephone ____________ 4 (*Festnetz*) before they are converted back to a radio signal for the final journey from base-station to their ____________ 5 (*Ziel*). Messages cannot be longer than 160 ____________ 6 (*Zeichen*) because they are ____________ 7 (*eingefügt*) into the control ____________ 8 (*Kanal*), which is ____________ 9 (*reserviert*) for ____________ 10 (*Verbindung*) between the base station and the mobile phone. The carrier's ____________ 11 (*Betriebskosten*) – ____________ 12 (*Speicherkapazität*) and ____________ 13 (*Mitarbeiter*) – are not affected by the ____________ 14 (*Menge*) of messages that are sent.

____ / 14 Punkte

Aufgabe 5

Beantworten Sie folgende Aufgaben zu den Absätzen D–F stichpunktartig auf Deutsch.

1 Welchen Weg geht eine SMS von einem Handy zu einem anderen? (*3 Punkte*)

– ____________

– ____________

– ____________

2 Wie lang darf eine SMS maximal sein? Warum? (*2 Punkte*)

– ____________ – ____________

3 Warum kann man sagen, dass eine SMS die Mobilfunkunternehmen nichts kostet?

____

4 Welche Fixkosten der Telekomunternehmen listet der Text auf? (*2 Punkte*)

– ____________ – ____________

____ / 8 Punkte

Jetzt können Sie sich trauen, die letzte Aufgabe zu lösen.

Aufgabe 6

Beantworten Sie folgende Aufgaben auf Deutsch.

1 Erklären Sie die Bedeutung der Überschrift zum Text.

____

____

2 Was bedeutet „one sees the carriers' pricing plans in an entirely new light" im Kontext? (Absatz G)

____

____

____ / 4 Punkte

Lesen Sie den Text und bearbeiten Sie die Aufgaben.

Even in skin-care advertising, youth prevails over age

Baby boomers are so last century.

A At least that is how a lot of the skin care companies see it. There may be tens of millions of baby boomers out there craving to renew their skin's youthful glow. But their children collectively represent an even bigger market for skin care regimens, and they will be around and spending on skin care for many decades to come.

"The cosmetics people are realizing that young people have plenty of money that they are perfectly willing to spend on lip glosses and creams," said Allan Mottus, a consultant to the beauty industry. "Now they are trying to figure out better ways to reach them."

B Few, if any, companies are actually abandoning the older crowd – anti-aging creams are big sellers. But increasingly, cosmetics companies are running parallel campaigns aimed at younger customers. The problem, the industry has discovered, is that the just-post-pimple crowd is pretty elusive. Young women are far less likely to shop in department stores than their mothers were. And department store cosmetics counters, with their fashionable consultants always ready to suggest products, have long been the retail venue of choice for introducing all but the cheapest products. So the companies are looking for new ways to bring those younger consumers in.

C In 2006, *Clinique*, which had been devoting about 90 per cent of its advertising budget to magazines and newspapers rarely read by those in their teens and 20s, began to advertise on MTV and other television shows aimed at a younger audience. It took its message to websites like *Facebook*. And it began demonstrating its new products on college campuses. Sales jumped almost 10 per cent in 2006, "and I really believe it is business from new young users," said Lynne Greene, president of *Clinique*. This year, less than 50 per cent of the ad budget will go to print.

Arden has changed its ways, too. It is advertising its new moisturizer in magazines that draw young readers. And it has also introduced a new three-in-one cleanser, for which it has mounted an internet-based campaign aimed at women in their mid-20s "who are really just getting interested in skin care," Park said. It has priced the product at $20 for 5 ounces – low for a department store brand, but more affordable for a younger buyer's budget.

D The companies have been fine-tuning the products and packaging as well. *Arden's* new cleanser is free of fragrance because *Arden's* market research showed that young women do not like scented skin products.

But it is in the marketing, not the actual products, that the industry's new fascination with youth comes through. None of the companies are following the old "hope in a jar" model – buy this cream and you will soon look like the beauty queen we have hired as its spokeswoman. Instead, they are using their websites and marketing materials to try to explain how the products work and why they are useful.

"This younger generation knows that a lot of the ingredients in the $50 jar are also in the $3 jar, but they also know that some products really can be differentiated on the basis of science," Park of *Arden* said.

E In fact, they also know that sometimes, common household items work just as well as fancy creams to solve skin problems. They were, after all, brought up by mothers who probably knew the trick of using cucumber slices to reduce puffiness around eyes.

571 words

baby boomer: someone born during the baby boom years, roughly 1945–1960.

adapted from: **International Herald Tribune**, 19 January, 2007

Aufgabe 1

Find English words in the text for these German words. Write them in the correct list below. (You have to complete the headings as well.)

Paragraph A
Berater/in • Creme • Kosmetika • Hautpflege • Lippenstift • Markt
Paragraph B
Firma • Kampagne • Konsument/in • Kunde • Produkt
Paragraph C
Feuchtigkeitscreme • Geschäft(e) • Marke • Reinigungsmilch • Verkaufszahlen • Werbeetat
Paragraphs D and E
Duft • ~~Marketing~~ • Marktforschung • parfümiert • Verpackung • Verschwollenheit • Zutat

Schönheit = ____________		Industrie = ____________	
		marketing	

______ / 25 Punkte

Aufgabe 2

Match the following headings to the paragraphs A–E in the text.

1 New marketing techniques
2 Young generation overtake their moms
3 Mom knows best
4 New advertising methods
5 Young women harder to reach

1	2	3	4	5

______ / 5 Punkte

Aufgabe 3

Beantworten Sie folgende Aufgaben stichpunktartig auf Deutsch.

1 Warum sind die Töchter der Babyboomer-Generation so interessant für die Hersteller von Kosmetika geworden? (*3 Punkte*)

– ____________
– ____________
– ____________

2 Warum finden die Kosmetikunternehmen es so schwer, junge Frauen für ihre Produkte zu gewinnen? (*2 Punkte*)

– ____________
– ____________

3 Welche Maßnahmen haben die Kosmetikfirmen ergriffen, um die jüngere Generation anzusprechen? (*4 Punkte*)

- ____
- ____
- ____
- ____

4 Was lehnen viele junge Frauen an Kosmetika ab? (*3 Punkte*)

- ____
- ____
- ____

5 Was hat die junge Generation von ihren Müttern gelernt?

____

____

_____ **/ 13 Punkte**

Aufgabe 4

Beantworten Sie folgende Aufgaben auf Deutsch.

1 Was meint die Autorin mit dem Satz „Baby boomers are so last century“? (Unterzeile)

____

____

____

2 Was bedeutet „craving to renew their skin's youthful glow“? (lines 4–5)

____

____

____

3 Was bedeutet „the just-post-pimple crowd is pretty elusive“ im Kontext? (lines 23–24)

____

____

____

4 Geben Sie sinngemäß die Hauptaussage von Absatz E wieder.

____

____

____

_____ **/ 8 Punkte**

Ich habe _____ Minuten für diesen Abschnitt gebraucht.

Ich habe _____ Mal ein Wörterbuch verwendet.

Ich habe _____ von 94 Punkten.

Jetzt kontrollieren Sie alle Antworten im Lösungsheft auf den Seiten 9/10.

STEP 8

Writing Skills 1: Describing and interpreting photos and cartoons
Topics: Youth, Society

In diesem STEP geht es darum, Fotos und Cartoons in Ihren eigenen Worten zu beschreiben, zu erklären oder zu interpretieren. Die Beschreibung sollte ungefähr zwei Drittel Ihres Textes füllen, die Erklärung bzw. Interpretation etwa ein Drittel.

Describing and interpreting photos and cartoons

Wie bei jeder Art schriftlicher Arbeit, sollten Sie nie einfach drauflosschreiben! Machen Sie immer Notizen, bevor Sie anfangen, die Aufgabe zu beantworten.

- **Notieren Sie alles, was Sie sehen:** Damit Sie nichts auslassen, können Sie bei Cartoons entweder von oben nach unten oder von links nach rechts arbeiten. Dies ist auch möglich bei Fotos, aber hier ist es oft besser, vom Vordergrund in den Hintergrund des Bildes zu arbeiten.
- **Fragen Sie sich, was das Motiv (*main part/subject*) des Bildes ist:** In einem Foto befindet sich dies meistens im Vordergrund des Bildes.
- **Überlegen Sie, was vorher passiert sein könnte:** Wie ist es zu dieser Situation gekommen?
- **Welche Stimmung erzeugt das Bild?** Ist es ernst, oberflächlich, humorvoll, traurig?
- **Welche Absicht hatte der Fotograf/die Fotografin?**
- **Schreiben Sie Ihre Antwort:** An Hand Ihrer Notizen können Sie jetzt eine vollständige Antwort schreiben.
- **Kontrollieren Sie Ihren Text:** Lesen Sie Ihre Arbeit noch einmal durch, um unnötige Fehler zu vermeiden.

Schauen Sie sich das Foto an und bearbeiten Sie die Aufgaben 1 und 2. (→ **Anhang 4**: Phrases for describing pictures, S. 55)

in the top left-hand corner

the subject of the photo

in the background

in the bottom right-hand corner

in the foreground

Aufgabe 1

Complete this description of the photo on page 36 using the words and phrases which are around it.

The photo shows a man and a woman in a car park. The main ______________ [1] of the photo is the woman in the ______________ [2]. She is walking away from the man. The man is in the ______________ [3], standing next to a row of cars. One of the cars might belong to him. ______________ [4] we can see a VW van and empty parking spaces. ______________ [5] there are lots of trees. It must be a hot day, because the woman is wearing a light top and flip-flops. We can also see her shadow ______________ [6].

____ / 6 Punkte

Aufgabe 2

Now complete this interpretation of the photo with the words in the box.

always • can assume • eye-catching feature • just • Looking at the way • might be • obviously • probably • think • wants to remind us

The woman is the most ______________ [1] of the photo. She is ______________ [2] walking away from the man and not looking back. ______________ [3] she is holding her hands out, we ______________ [4] that she is angry with the man. I ______________ [5] that the car park ______________ [6] at a motorway service station. It is ______________ [7] a very hot day and they have ______________ [8] had an argument in the car. The photographer ______________ [9] that men and women do not ______________ [10] get on with each other.

____ / 10 Punkte

More about interpreting cartoons

Cartoons werden in Zeitungen und Zeitschriften abgedruckt, daher haben sie oft einen Bezug zu einem aktuellen Thema: entweder die gegenwärtige politische Situation, gesellschaftliche Trends und Ereignisse, oder eine kontroverse soziale Frage. Sie können einen Cartoon so beschreiben, wie Sie es für Fotos gelernt haben. Nur müssen Sie auf die folgenden Besonderheiten von Cartoons achten:

- **Sprechblasen (*speech bubbles*), Bildunterschriften (*captions*), Etiketten (*labels*):** *cartoonists* verwenden oft diese Hilfsmittel, und sie müssen auch einen Platz in Ihrer Beschreibung finden.
- **Symbole:** Oft steht ein Objekt (wie z. B. eine Flagge) für eine Idee, eine Organisation oder ein Land.
- **Karikatur:** Bei einer *caricature* wird ein körperliches Merkmal übertrieben dargestellt.
- **Absicht:** Bei der Beschreibung eines Cartoons gilt es, die Absicht (*point*) zu erkennen und abschließend zu erläutern.

Die Tipps, wie man ein Bild beschreibt, gelten auch für Cartoons, aber bei der Interpretation von Cartoons muss man ein paar andere Details beachten.

Schauen Sie sich diese Cartoons an und bearbeiten Sie die Aufgaben 3 und 4.

Aufgabe 3

Use the words in the first column to label the cartoons below.

caption	words or sentence that summarize(s) the message of the cartoon
caricature	used to exaggerate one or more physical features of a person
label	word or words that say(s) exactly who or what something is
sign	words that give information about something
speech bubble	something that a character says or thinks (thought bubble)
symbol	an image used to represent an idea

____ / 6 Punkte

Barack Obama ← 1 ____

2 ____

3 ____

4 ____

5 ____

CELL HELL ← 6 ____

Wenn Sie ein Bild oder einen Cartoon beschreiben, benutzen Sie **the present tense**. Für Ereignisse, die offensichtlich gerade im Gange sind, verwenden Sie **the present progressive**. Ansonsten sollten Sie **the present simple** benutzen. Natürlich sind andere Zeiten, wie z. B. **present perfect** oder **will-future** möglich, je nach dem Sinn Ihres Textes.

____ / 16 Punkte

Aufgabe 4

Complete this description of the cartoon "Cell Hell". Cross out the wrong form of the verbs. The first one has been done for you.

The illustration shows/~~is showing~~ [1] a man who had/has [2] just arrived in hell. There was/is [3] a sign which says/is saying [4] "Welcome to hell" and the devil sits/is sitting [5] at a reception desk. There are/were [6] red flames in the background and we can/could [7] also see the roof of the cave. The man looks/is looking [8] anxiously at his mobile phone and in a speech bubble he said/says [9]: "Oh no! No signal!!" The caption reads/is reading [10] "Cell hell". Americans call/are calling [11] their mobile phones "cellphones".

The cartoonist makes/is making [12] fun of the fact that mobile phones are/will be [13] so important in our lives. The man wasn't/isn't [14] worried that he had/has [15] gone to hell. His main concern is/will be [16] that he wasn't/won't be [17] able to use his phone there.

PRACTICE 8

Bearbeiten Sie die Aufgaben 1–3.
(→ **Anhang 4**: Phrases for describing pictures, S. 55)

Aufgabe 1

Complete the description of this photo. Put the verbs in brackets into the most suitable tense.

This photo ______________[1] (show) a young woman who ______________[2] (lean) against the wall of a building. She ______________[3] (hold) her head with one hand. In the other hand she ______________[4] (have) a bottle of beer. We ______________[5] (not/see) her face and we ______________[6] (not/know) which town or city she ______________[7] (be) in, but it ______________[8] (seem) to be dark. A man ______________[9] (bend) over next to her. It ______________[10] (look) as if he ______________[11] (help) her.

I think the photographer ______________[12] (want) to show the effects of binge-drinking. The young woman ______________[13] (probably/be) out with some friends and ______________[14] (drink) too much. Now she ______________[15] (feel) sick and ______________[16] (need) help to get home.

_____ / 16 Punkte

Aufgabe 2

Look at this photo and complete the notes. The words in the box might help you.

alone • feel ill • friends left her • head • knees • slumped (*zusammengesackt*) • spilt liquid • unknown town or city

Main subject of photo: ______________

Where is she? ______________

How old is subject? ______________

Other people in photo? ______________

Time of photo? ______________

Other features in photo? ______________

Aim of photographer? ______________

Explanation of situation? ______________

_____ / 8 Punkte

Aufgabe 3

Now describe what you see in the photo at the bottom of page 39 and explain the situation. Write about 80–100 words.

____

____

____

____

____

____

____

_____ / 20 Punkte

Bearbeiten Sie die Aufgaben 4–6.
(→ **Anhang 4**: Phrases for describing pictures, S. 55)

Aufgabe 4

Look at the cartoon and put the sentences into the correct order to describe it. The first one has been done for you.

	Behind him, in the bottom right-hand corner, there is a ball, but he is not interested in it.
	As a result, it is not surprising that the boy spends all his time inside.
	She is standing in the doorway looking crossly at the boy.
1	This cartoon shows a typical boy's bedroom.
	In the background we can see the boy's mother.
	He is only interested in the internet and she is only worried about the expensive computer.
	In a speech bubble she says, "Nine hours in a row on the internet! Do you think that's good for your computer?"
	Both the boy and the mother are overweight.
	A boy is sitting at his computer.

_____ / 8 Punkte

Aufgabe 5

Describe and analyse this cartoon. Base your description on the sentences in exercise 4. Use the notes to help you analyse the cartoon.

- cartoonist / make / point / internet / not always help people / communicate / each other
- boy / addicted / weblog
- mother / probably not know / what / weblog is

This cartoon shows ____

A boy ____

____.

Behind him, ____

____.

In the background ______________________________

______________________________.

She ______________________________

______________________________.

In a speech bubble ______________________________

______________________________.

The cartoonist is ______________________________

______________________________.

The boy is ______________________________

______________________________.

____ / 15 Punkte

Aufgabe 6

Describe this cartoon and explain the point the cartoonist is making. Write 80–100 words. Once again, the notes will help you.

- man / visit / son / prison
- left / young man / prison cell
- look / unhappy
- middle / man / talk / him
- speech bubble
- behind / right / another young man / cell
- speech bubble
- cartoonist / satirize / parents / not really know / children / very well
- father / obviously / not spent / much time / son

____

____

____

____

____

____

____

____

____

____

____ / 20 Punkte

Ich habe ____ Minuten für diesen Abschnitt gebraucht.

Ich habe ____ Mal ein Wörterbuch verwendet.

Ich habe ____ von 125 Punkten.

Jetzt kontrollieren Sie alle Antworten im Lösungsheft auf den Seiten 11/12.

In diesem STEP geht es darum, Diagramme und Statistiken in Ihren eigenen Worten zu beschreiben und zu interpretieren. Diagramme sind bildliche Darstellungen von Zahlen (Statistiken); man unterscheidet Liniendiagramme (**line graphs**), Balkendiagramme (**bar charts**) und Kreisdiagramme (**pie charts**). Statistiken können auch in Form einer Tabelle (**table**) präsentiert werden.

Describing graphs and statistics

Wie bei jeder Art schriftlicher Arbeit sollten Sie nie einfach drauflosschreiben! Machen Sie immer Notizen, bevor Sie anfangen, die Aufgabe zu beantworten. Schauen Sie sich zuerst die wichtigsten Teile des Diagrammes an:

- **Titel:** Er sagt Ihnen, worum es geht.
- **Achsen:** Hier wird normalerweise vorgegeben, in welchen Einheiten (y-Achse) und über welchen Zeitraum (x-Achse) gemessen wurde.
- **Legenden (*labels*):** Sie verdeutlichen, um welche Gruppen oder Teilwerte es sich handelt.
- **Zahlen:** In welche Richtung gehen die Trends? Gibt es markante Unterschiede? Hat es große Veränderungen gegeben?

Schließlich sollten Sie **Schlussfolgerungen** aus den Informationen ziehen. Vielleicht können Sie Ihre Antwort mit weiteren Informationen aus dem Unterricht untermauern.

Schreiben Sie nun Ihre Antwort anhand Ihrer Notizen und lesen Sie Ihre Arbeit noch einmal durch, um unnötige Fehler zu vermeiden.

Schauen Sie sich die Diagramme an und bearbeiten Sie die Aufgaben.
(→ **Anhang 5**: Phrases for describing graphs and statistics, S. 55)

Aufgabe 1

Read the text and write the highlighted words in the correct place on the diagrams below.

Graphs are used to show statistics in a visual form that is easier to understand than just a table of figures. A line graph usually has an x-axis and a y-axis. Points on the graph are joined together by lines that clearly show a trend over a period of time. The lines usually have a label, as well as a different colour, so that you can easily see which one is which. A bar chart consists of columns or bars that can be used to clearly compare different sets of information. A pie chart is a circle that is divided into different segments. It is usually used to show different groups as a percentage of a larger group.

1 ____________________

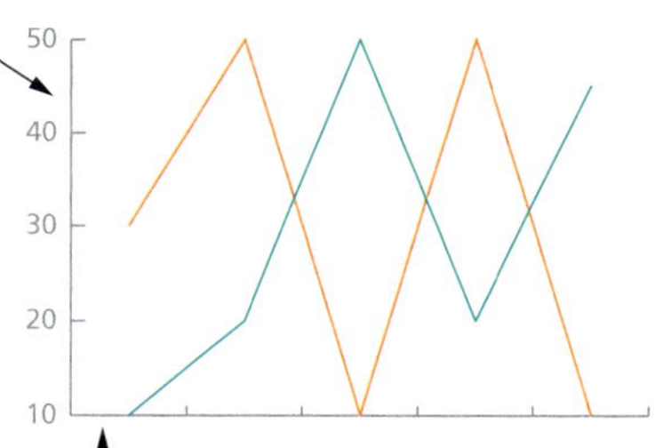

2 ____________________

3 ____________________

4 ____________________

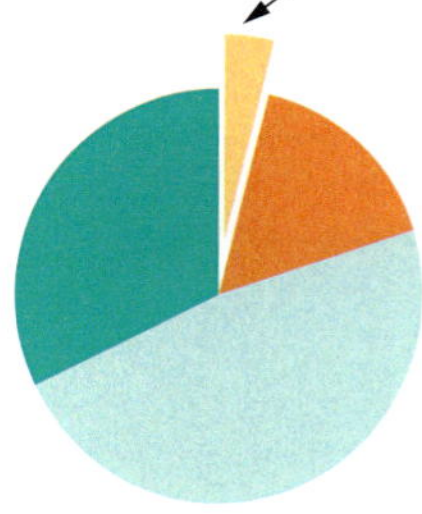

5 ____________________

2000	2009
5	7.5
10	7.5
...	...

6 ____________________

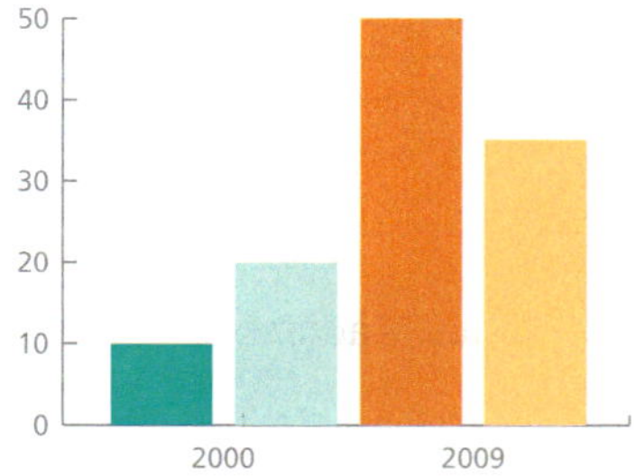

7 ____________________

____ / 7 Punkte

Aufgabe 2

Look at the graph and complete the description below.

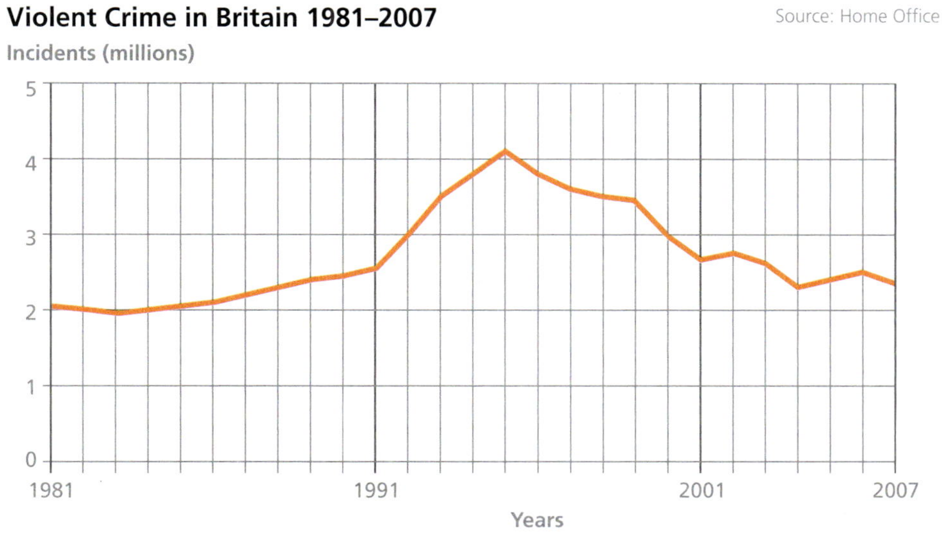

This graph shows trends in ____________________[1] between __________[2] and __________[3]. On the ______________[4] you can see the years from 1981 to 2007. The ______________[5] displays the number of ______________[6] (*Vorfälle*) in ______________[7].

The number of violent crimes was just over ______________[8] million in 1981. It dropped slightly up to __________[9] then climbed gradually until __________[10]. There was a steep rise up to __________[11], before the figures began to decline again. They decreased steadily until __________[12], when they flattened off. Another steady decrease followed until __________[13], before there was another sharp increase up to __________[14]. From 2006 to __________[15] there was a slight drop in violent crimes.

_____ / 15 Punkte

Aufgabe 3

Look at the text in exercise 2 and answer these questions.

1 Which tense do you use to describe what the graph is about? (first paragraph)

____

2 Which tense do you use to describe trends in the graph? (second paragraph)

____

3 What part of speech are the highlighted words?
a) ☐ adjective + verb b) ☐ adjective + noun c) ☐ adverb + verb

4 What part of speech are the highlighted words?
a) ☐ noun + adjective b) ☐ verb + adjective c) ☐ verb + adverb

_____ / 4 Punkte

Man kann einen Trend entweder mit Verb + Adverb oder Adjektiv + Substantiv beschreiben. Das Verb ist normalerweise im **simple past**.

Aufgabe 4

Rewrite these sentences, using the examples in the box to help you.

There was a dramatic drop in the numbers. → The numbers dropped dramatically.

The figures declined steeply. → There was a steep decline in the figures.

There was a slight drop in the figures from 1981 to 1983.

The figures ______________________________ 1 from 1981 to 1983.

The figures rose steadily from 1983 to 1991.

There was ____________________ 2 in the figures ______________ 3.

The number of violent crimes increased sharply up to 1995.

There was ______________________________ 4 the number of violent

crimes ________________ 5.

There was a gradual fall in violent crime from 1995 to 2001.

____ 6 1995 to 2001.

There was a sudden climb in incidents of violent crime from 2005 to 2006.

____ 7

The numbers decreased slowly from 2006 to 2007.

____ 8

_____ / 8 Punkte

Aufgabe 5

Compare these two graphs. Write about 200 words.

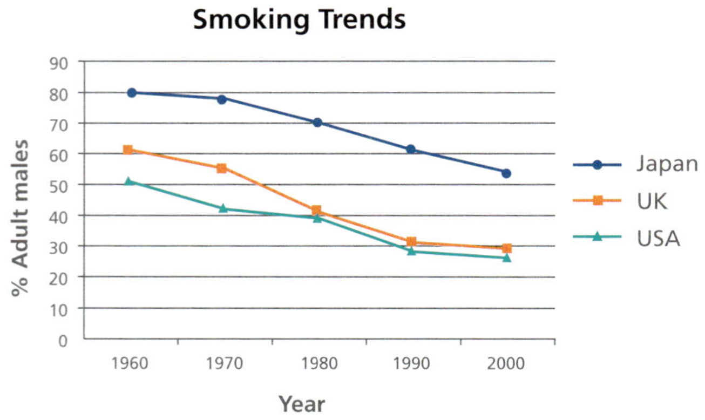

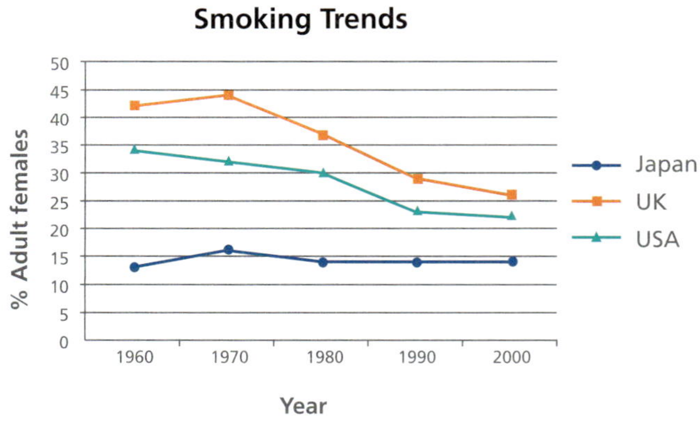

____

____

____

____

____

____

____

____

_____ / 20 Punkte

PRACTICE 9

Aufgabe 1

Look at this bar chart then find the sentences that describe it in the word maze.

Bearbeiten Sie die Aufgaben.
(→ **Anhang 5**: Phrases for describing graphs and statistics, S. 55)

Internet users in the world by geographic regions

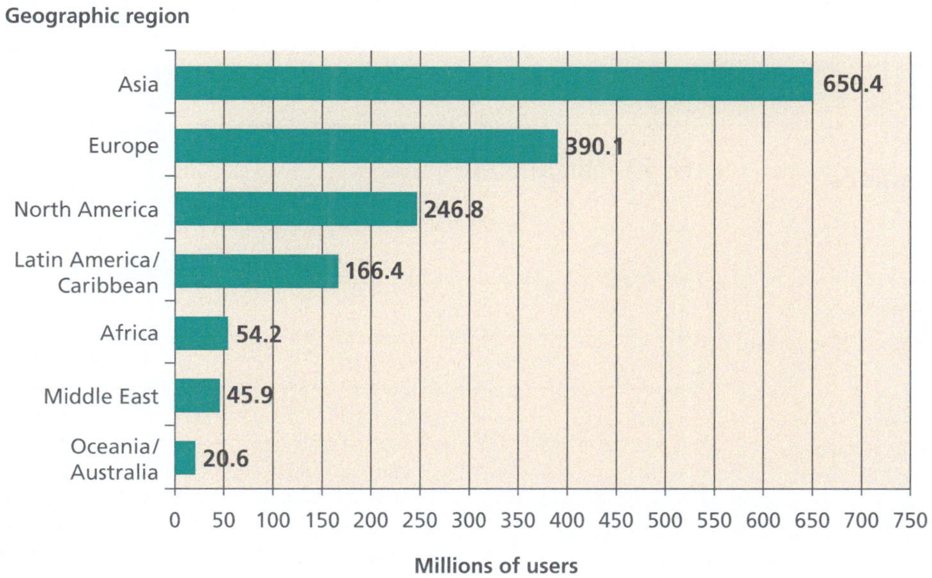

START ▼

This	bar	in	the	world.	The
shows	chart	internet	the	gives	y-axis
how	use	the	number	x-axis	shows
many	people	users	of	The	the
America	North	in	millions.	regions.	geographic
and	Europe.	in	There	are	over
Latin	America	million	followed	Asia,	650
the	are	390.1	by	in	million
next	to	the	chart,	users	internet
two	According	are	there	internet	users
largest	groups.	only	internet	users	in
with	Oceania/Australia	54.2	million	and	Africa
20.6	is	The	East.	45.9	million
million.	group	smallest	Middle	the	in

FINISH

This bar chart shows how many ______

______ / 12 Punkte

REMEMBER!

Im Englischen schreibt man „3.4%" (three point four per cent), nicht „3,4%".

Aufgabe 2

Use the sentences from exercise 1 to help you write a description of this pie chart. The words in the box will also help you.

percentage of (*Prozentsatz*) • come from • be from • be divided into

This pie chart shows ____.

World internet users by geographic regions

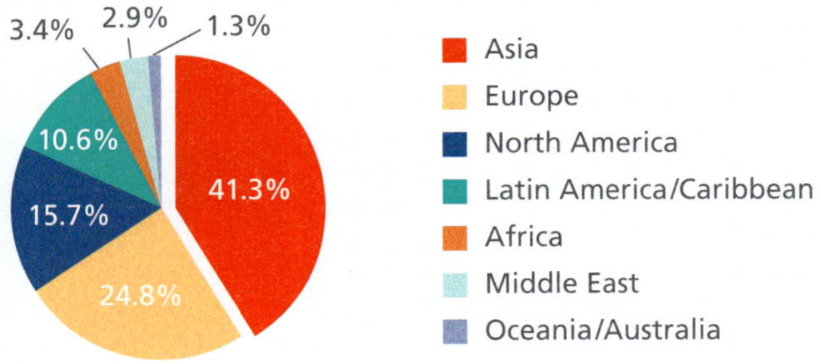

The pie chart is ____.

The largest ____

_____ / 12 Punkte

Aufgabe 3

Look at this bar chart and the pie chart in exercise 2 and complete the sentences.

World internet access by geographic regions

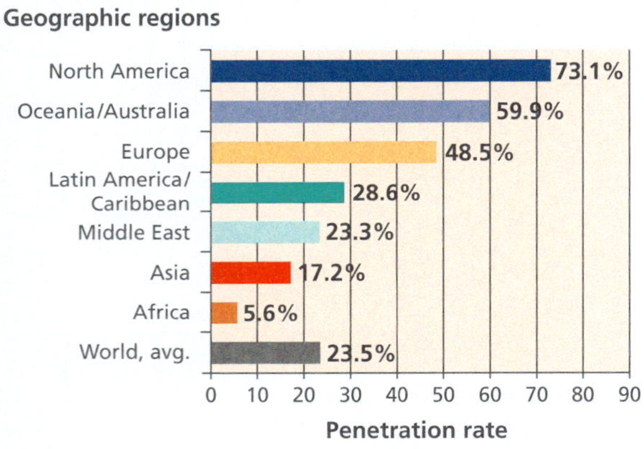

1 The ________________ (large) group of internet users come from Asia, but internet access (*Zugang/Verbreitung*) in Asia is ________________ (not/high) in North America.

2 Oceania/Australia has ________________ (small) number of internet users, but the second ________________ (high) rate of internet access. Only North America is ________________ (high).

3 Africa has ________________ (low) rate of internet access, but the number of internet users is ________________ (big) in the Middle East.

4 The number of internet users in Latin America is ________________ (not/big) in North America.

5 Europe has the second ________________ (large) number of internet users, but the rate of internet access is ________________ (small) in Oceania/Australia.

_____ / 10 Punkte

Aufgabe 4

Look at the two charts in exercises 2 and 3 and write sentences from these notes.

internet users

1 / more / Europe / North America

____

2 / fewer / Latin America / North America

____

3 / most / Asia

____

4 / least number of / come from / Oceania/Australia

____

internet access

5 / Oceania/Australia / about 10% more / Europe

____

6 / Europe / twice / high / Middle East

____

7 / Latin America / about 20% less / Europe

____

8 / Middle East / about / same / world average

____

____ /8 Punkte

Aufgabe 5

Look at the two charts in exercises 2 and 3. Compare internet users and internet access and give reasons why they are different. Write three sentences for each of the following geographic regions. The example will help you.

Asia has the highest number of internet users with 41.3% of the total. However, internet access in Asia is the second lowest of all the geographic regions, with only 17.2%. This is probably because Asia has such a large population but is not so economically developed.

1 Oceania/Australia ______________________________

____

____

____

2 Africa ______________________________

____

____

____

3 North America ______________________________

____

____

____

____

____ /9 Punkte

Ich habe ____ Minuten für diesen Abschnitt gebraucht.

Ich habe ____ Mal ein Wörterbuch verwendet.

Ich habe ____ von 105 Punkten.

Jetzt kontrollieren Sie alle Antworten im Lösungsheft auf den Seiten 12–14.

STEP 10

Writing Skills 3: Writing a composition
Topics: Media, Sport

Das Schwierigste kommt zuletzt: einen Aufsatz zu einem vorgegebenen Thema mit Ihren eigenen Ideen zu schreiben. Hier die wichtigsten zwei Aufsatzarten:

1) Sie sollen Ihre Meinung zum Thema formulieren und mit Argumenten belegen (**opinion composition**);

2) Sie sollen das Für und Wider (**pros and cons**) zu einem Thema erörtern (**for and against composition**) und sich dann dazu äußern.

Writing a composition

Ein guter Aufsatz steht auf drei Stützen, wie ein Hocker mit drei Beinen. Alle drei Stützen sind gleich wichtig, sobald eine fehlt, bricht das Ganze zusammen. Die drei Stützen sind:
1 Inhalt (logisch aneinander gereihte Argumente);
2 Stil (*linking words/phrases*, Wortschatz, anspruchsvolle Strukturen);
3 Sprache (weitgehend fehlerfreies Englisch).

Befolgen Sie diese Schritte, damit Ihre Aufsätze stark und „sitzfest" werden.

- **Welche Art von Aufsatz?** Überlegen Sie zuerst, welche Art von Aufsatz (1 oder 2) verlangt wird. Sie könnten Punkte verlieren, wenn z. B. Ihre Meinung in einer „opinion composition" fehlt.
- **Sammeln Sie Ideen:** Notieren Sie alles, was Sie über das Thema wissen (und Ihre eigenen Ideen); Sie können dies an Hand einer *mind map* zeichnen, oder als formlose Notizen aufschreiben.
- **Was meinen Sie?** Überlegen Sie, wie Sie zu dem Thema stehen, wenn danach gefragt wird.
- **Ordnen Sie Ihre Gedanken:** Bringen Sie nun Ihre Ideen in eine strukturierte Form, die zu der Themenstellung passt.

Es gibt verschiedene Möglichkeiten, einen Aufsatz zu gliedern. Schauen Sie sich diese Gliederungshilfe an und bearbeiten Sie Aufgabe 1.

Opinion composition	For and against composition
Introduction – introduce the topic (– give your opinion, if you want)	Introduction – introduce the topic (– explain how you are going to deal with the topic, if you want)
Main body of the text – present arguments supporting your opinion OR – start with one or more counter-arguments (*Gegenargument*) first, then present your arguments – always keep your most convincing argument till last	Main body of the text – present arguments "for" then arguments "against" OR – present arguments "against" then arguments "for" OR – present each argument followed by a counter-argument (*Gegenargument*)
Conclusion – state your opinion, without adding any new arguments	Conclusion – say whether you support one position or the other, if you want OR – say that the topic is too complicated for you to decide
Key phrases 1 _____ 2 _____ 3 _____ 4 _____ 5 _____ 6 _____ 7 _____	Key phrases 1 _____ 2 _____ 3 _____ 4 _____ 5 _____ 6 _____ 7 _____

Aufgabe 1

Look at the following composition tasks. The underlined phrases show whether the task requires an 'opinion composition' or a 'for and against composition'. Write the key phrases in the table (page 48). Two phrases can go in either list.

1 Reality TV shows that humiliate their candidates should be banned. Discuss this idea.
2 Some politicians want to ban all forms of tobacco consumption. Do you agree with them?
3 'Sports stars who use steroids to enhance their performance should be banned for life.' Give your opinion on this idea.
4 Newspapers and magazines should not be allowed to publish photos of stars without their consent. Do you think this demand is justified?
5 'Smokers should pay more for their health care.' Comment on this suggestion.
6 'The use of mobile phones should be banned in all public places, including buses and trains.' What are the main arguments for and against such a course of action?
7 'Top bank managers earn far too much money.' Do you agree or disagree with this statement.

____ / 7 Punkte

Aufgabe 2

Use ideas from the box to complete this composition plan.

Sie sollten versuchen, Ihre Argumente mit Erklärungen oder Beispielen zu unterstützen.

candidates don't have to go on the show • degrading for candidates • form of censorship • freedom of choice for viewer • people soon get bored • pure entertainment • should they be banned? • viewing figures important • viewers decide what is shown on TV • who decides what is good/bad TV?

Reality TV shows that humiliate their candidates should be banned. Discuss this idea in about 200 words.

For and against composition

Introduction

some shows humiliate candidates, ____________

Main part 1 – For

no information value, ____________

____________, *do unpleasant tasks*

____________, *producers looking for new 'thrills'*

Main part 2 – Against

____________, *want to be on show*

____________, *no one has to watch*

____________ ____________

Conclusion

____________ ____________

____ / 10 Punkte

Aufgabe 3

Put the paragraphs of this finished composition in the correct order.

A	It is often said that reality TV shows are pure entertainment and don't inform their audiences in any way. More importantly, some of them degrade and humiliate the candidates by making them do unpleasant tasks, like eat worms or ants. Take for example the tasks the candidates on 'jungle' shows have to complete. In addition, the shows are competing with each other for viewers and therefore the producers always have to think of new 'thrills' to attract an audience.
B	My own point of view is that the viewers decide what is shown on TV and that people will soon get bored of watching shows if they are not interesting as well as entertaining.
C	Some people claim that reality TV shows are humiliating for the candidates, but would it really be right to ban something that a lot of people enjoy watching?
D	Despite this, there are always enough candidates who want to join the shows and nobody forces them to take part. What is more, nobody is forced to watch any of these shows and viewers can switch off the TV or change channels when they want to. The last point I'd like to mention is that a ban on reality TV shows would be a form of censorship and who would decide which shows are degrading and which are not?

1	2	3	4

_____ /4 Punkte

Aufgabe 4

Sie dürfen nicht vergessen, Ihre Argumente richtig zu verbinden. (→ **Anhang 6**: Phrases for writing compositions, S. 56)

Which phrase links the ideas/arguments best. Cross out the phrases that don't fit. Then answer the question at the end.

It is common knowledge that / ~~The first thing to point out is that~~ top football stars earn a lot of money. In other words / I personally believe that [1] it is unfair for a football player to earn more in a week than most people do in a year.

Another argument is that / The first thing to point out is that [2] tickets for league matches are expensive, although / for example [3] the clubs earn a lot of money from sponsorship and pay TV deals. The reason for this is that / What is more [4] the clubs spend too much money on their players' salaries. We must also take into account that / Last but not least [5] the enormous salaries for top football stars mean that only the richest clubs can afford the best players and in addition / therefore [6] the smaller clubs have no chance to keep or even sign players such as Cristiano Ronaldo or Lionel Messi. The last point I'd like to make is that / On the contrary [7] there are more important jobs that contribute much more to society than sportspeople. In other words / Take for example [8] a nurse, working long hours caring for people, who would have to work six years to earn what a top footballer earns in one week.

In my opinion / To sum up [9], I'm convinced that there should be a limit to how much footballers earn. I have no doubt that / On the other hand [10] they would still want to play football even if they didn't earn quite as much money.

What type of composition is it? Tick the correct box.

☐ Opinion composition ☐ For and against composition

_____ /11 Punkte

PRACTICE 10

Aufgabe 1

Complete this composition with the English equivalent of the German phrases in brackets.

Bearbeiten Sie die Aufgaben.
(→ **Anhang 6**: Phrases for writing compositions, S. 56)

Newspapers and magazines should not be allowed to publish photos of stars without their consent. Do you think this demand is justified?

____________________[1] (*Es ist allgemein bekannt, dass …*) pop and film stars are often chased by paparazzi outside restaurants or even their homes. ____________________[2] (*Ich habe keine Zweifel, dass …*) this is harmless, ________________[3] (*obwohl*) it does annoy the stars sometimes.

____________________[4] (*Zunächst [ist zu sagen, dass …]*), famous people often argue that they have a right to privacy like everyone else; ____________________[5] (*sie behaupten*) that the photographers wouldn't like photos of themselves in their pyjamas on the front page of a newspaper. ____________________[6] (*Was noch wichtiger ist*), they say that their families are affected as well. Their children, ________________[7] (*im Besonderen*), suffer if they are hounded by the press all the time. ____________________[8] (*Ein anderes Argument*) is that they are more exposed to dangers, ________________[9] (*wie zum Beispiel*) kidnapping, blackmail or stalking, than normal citizens.

____________________[10] (*Trotz alledem*), I believe that the lives of famous people are of interest to the public and that we should have a chance to see how they live.

____________________[11] (*Und wir dürfen nicht vergessen*) that most stars don't have a problem with photographers and accept the press as part of their job. ________________[12] (*Zuletzt*), there are also enough famous people who want publicity, to make sure that they stay "in the public eye" for their careers.

____________________[13] (*Zusammenfassend*), I think that the paparazzi are the price stars have to pay for their fame. ____________________[14] (*Ich bin überzeugt, dass …*) it is a price most of them are happy to pay, so long as they are not put in danger.

_____ **/ 14 Punkte**

Aufgabe 2

Use the arguments in the composition in exercise 1 to complete this essay plan. You need one argument and one explanation/example for each bullet point.

Introduction
- paparazzi harmless (argument); sometimes annoys stars (explanation)

For
- ______________________ – ______________________
- ______________________ – ______________________
- ______________________ – ______________________

Against
- ______________________ – ______________________
- ______________________ – ______________________
- ______________________ – ______________________

Conclusion
- ______________________ – ______________________
- ______________________ – ______________________

____ / 16 Punkte

Aufgabe 3

Put these sentences from a finished composition into the right order. The first one has been done for you.

'Sports stars who use steroids to enhance their performance should be banned for life.' Give your opinion on this statement in about 200 words.

1	Every time there is a major sporting event, such as the Olympic Games or the Tour de France, there are always stories about doping in the news.
	In my opinion they should be banned for two years, after which they should be given a second chance.
	There is no doubt in my mind that sports stars who use steroids should be banned, but I'm not so sure that they should be banned for life.
	Last but not least, they are cheating all the spectators and fans who support them, which ruins the appeal of the sport for the future.
	The athletes that are caught by drugs test usually say that it is the pressure to win that forces them to use steroids, particularly if they are trying to come back after an injury.
	What is more, they are cheating their fellow competitors, and if they win, the financial gains they make are nothing more than fraud.
	Furthermore, they argue that if they don't take performance-enhancing drugs, they will have no chance to compete at the highest level.
	This argument is simply nonsense: just think of the damage they are doing to their own bodies, as well as the bad example they are setting for young people who want to start a career in sports.
	Taking everything into account, no one can seriously doubt that athletes who take drugs/steroids deserve to be banned.

____ / 8 Punkte

Aufgabe 4

Complete the composition, using the notes below.

'The use of mobile phones should be banned in all public places, including buses and trains.' What are the main arguments for and against such a course of action?

Introduction
annoying behaviour – really need ban?

For
mobile phones in public = nuisance
impossible to read, think, talk while sb. on phone
mobiles adds to noise of modern life, e.g. traffic, loud music, roadworks, etc. = health hazard
mobile in public = bad manners; should respect privacy other passengers

Against
important part of our life: need make appointments / keep in contact with friends
so many aspects lives are controlled, e.g. smoking public, not need more laws
not practical to enforce ban; thousands passengers become criminals

Conclusion
use in public places should be reduced; learn respect privacy / other travellers

Everyone has sat next to someone in a bus or train who talked loudly into their mobile phone for the whole journey. This is ______________________________

____.

Those who support this suggestion maintain that ______________________________

______________________________. They say that ______________________________

____.

In addition, they believe that ______________________________

____.

Furthermore, they claim that ______________________________

____.

On the other hand, we must not forget that ______________________________

____.

We must also take into account that ______________________________

____.

The most important problem, however, is that ______________________________

____.

All in all, I am of the opinion that ______________________________

______________________________ but this will only be possible if people

____.

_____ / 10 Punkte

Ich habe _____ Minuten für diesen Abschnitt gebraucht.

Ich habe _____ Mal ein Wörterbuch verwendet.

Ich habe _____ von 80 Punkten.

Jetzt kontrollieren Sie alle Antworten im Lösungsheft auf den Seiten 14/15.

1 WORD BUILDING

Prefixes (Vorsilben)
Prefixes can change the meaning of a word.

anti-	'against'	clockwise → anticlockwise
co-	'together'	operate → co-operate
inter-	'between'	national → international
sub-	'under' / 'below'	standard → substandard
super-	'above' / 'over'	power → superpower
trans-	'across'	form → transform
dis-	'not' / 'opposite'	agree → disagree
in-		correct → incorrect
im-		possible → impossible
ir-		responsible → irresponsible
un-		friendly → unfriendly
mis-	'not correctly'	understand → misunderstand
re-	'again'	discover → rediscover

Suffixes (Nachsilben)
Suffixes can change a word from one word class to another.

Verbs → nouns

Verb	Suffix	Noun
organize	-ation	organization
express	-ion	expression
bake	-er	baker
begin	-ing	beginning
argue	-ment	argument

Verbs → adjectives

Verb	Suffix	Adjective
advise	-able	advisable
care	-ing	caring

Nouns → adjectives

Noun	Suffix	Adjective
continent	-al	continental
beauty	-ful	beautiful
day	-ly	daily
hunger	-ry	hungry

Adjectives → nouns

Adjective	Suffix	Noun
stupid	-ity	stupidity
happy	-ness	happiness

Adjectives → adverbs

Adjective	Suffix	Noun
awful	-ly	awfully
democratic	-ally	democratically

2 VERBS WITH TO-INFINITIVE; VERBS WITH -ING FORM

Verbs with to-infinitive

agree	hope	plan	tell
choose	learn	pretend	threaten
decide	manage	promise	want
expect	mean	refuse	

Verbs with -ing form

admit	enjoy	mind	suggest
avoid	finish	miss	
consider	imagine	practise	
deny	mention	risk	

Verbs with to-infinitive/-ing form (no difference in meaning)

begin	continue	intend	start
hate*	like*	love*	prefer*

Auf *hate, like, love* und *prefer* können *to-infinitive* oder *-ing form* folgen. Auf *would hate, would like, would love* und *would prefer* folgt immer der *to-infinitive*.

Verbs with to-infinitive/-ing form (difference in meaning)

Was auf diese Verben folgt, hängt davon ab, in welchem Sinn sie verwendet werden.

forget (+ -ing form)	*vergessen, etwas gemacht zu haben*
forget (+ to-infinitive)	*vergessen, etwas zu tun*
remember (+ -ing form)	*sich erinnern, etwas gemacht zu haben*
remember (+ to-infinitive)	*sich erinnern, etwas zu tun*
stop (+ -ing form)	*aufhören, etwas zu tun*
stop (+ to-infinitive)	*anhalten, um etwas anderes zu tun*
try (+ -ing form)	*etwas ausprobieren*
try (+ to-infinitive)	*sich anstrengen, etwas zu tun*

3 PHRASAL VERBS

call off	*absagen*
carry on	*weitermachen*
find out	*herausfinden*
get off	*ab-/aussteigen*
get on	*auf-/einsteigen*
get on with	*auskommen mit*
give in	*nachgeben*
give up	*aufgeben*
go on	*weitermachen*
hear about	*hören von*
look after	*sorgen für*
look for	*suchen*
look forward to	*sich auf etwas freuen*
look up	*nachschlagen*
pick up	*mitnehmen*
point out	*hinweisen*
put up	*aufstellen*
put up with	*sich abfinden mit*
set off	*aufbrechen nach*
talk to	*reden mit*
think about	*nachdenken*
think of	*denken über/an*
think up	*ausdenken*
turn around	*umdrehen*
turn down	*ablehnen*
turn into	*sich verwandeln*
turn off	*ausmachen/-schalten*
turn out	*sich herausstellen*
turn up	*auftauchen, erscheinen*
wait for	*warten*

4 PHRASES FOR DESCRIBING PICTURES

Describing the picture/cartoon
The photo/cartoon shows / focuses on ...
The photo/cartoon depicts ...
The main subject of the photo/cartoon is ...
... is the most eye-catching feature of the photo/cartoon.

At the front of the photo/cartoon there is ...
At the left/right we can see ...
At the top right / bottom left there is ...
In the middle of the picture/cartoon ... /
In the background you can see ...
The ... in the background isn't in focus / is out of focus.
We can't see ...

There is a caption under the illustration that says, "..."
There is a speech bubble which reads, "..."
In a speech bubble he/she says, "..."

Interpreting the picture/cartoon
I think that ...
I believe that ...
Looking at ... , we can assume that ...
What I find interesting about the photo is that ...

This picture is meant to show us ...
The photographer wants to remind us ...
The aim of the photo is to ...
The picture shows the effects of ...

The cartoonist is making the point that ...
The cartoonist is making fun of the fact that ...
The cartoonist is satirizing the fact that ...

As a result ...
obviously/probably/possibly/...
just

5 PHRASES FOR DESCRIBING GRAPHS AND STATISTICS

Saying what the graph is about
This line graph shows trends in ...
This bar chart shows/depicts ...
The pie chart is divided into ...

On the x-axis/y-axis you can see ...
The x-axis/y-axis shows/gives/displays the number of ...
in (thousands/millions/percent).

Describing trends

The number of ...	dropped slightly	
	decreased steadily	
	fell suddenly	
There was ...	a slight drop	in the number of ...
	a steady decrease	
	a sudden fall	
The number of ...	rose sharply	
	increased gradually	
	climbed steeply	
There was ...	a sharp rise	in the number of ...
	a gradual increase	
	a steep climb	

According to the chart, ...
The chart shows that ...
The number of ... remained the same / didn't change from 2000 to 2008.
The figures fluctuated between 2000 and 2008.

Comparing figures
... is bigger/larger/smaller than ...
... is the (second) largest/smallest of the ...
... is (not) as high/low as ...
... is (about) the same as ...
There are more/fewer ... in (Europe) than in (Asia).
The most/least ... are/come from ...
... is about (10) % more/less than in ...
... is (twice) as big as in ...

6 PHRASES FOR WRITING COMPOSITIONS

Introducing a topic
Everyone knows that ...
It is common knowledge that ...
It is often said that ...
Some people claim that ...

Linking arguments
The first thing to point out is that ...
We must also take into account that ...
And we must not forget that ...
The most important problem is (that) ...
Another argument is (that) ...
In addition, ...
What is more, ...
Furthermore, ...
Above all, ...
Firstly/Secondly/Thirdly, ...
Finally, ...
Last but not least, ...
The last point I'd like to mention is ...

Giving examples
(Take) for example ...
for instance ...
such as ...
just think of ...
particularly / in particular ...

Contrasting ideas
although ...
Despite this, ...
in spite of (all this) ...
on the other hand ...
on the contrary ...

Explaining consequences
Therefore ...
Consequently...
For that reason ...

Expressing your opinion
I have no doubt that ...
I'm of the opinion that ...
I'm convinced/sure that ...
I personally believe that ...
There's no doubt in my mind that ...
No one can seriously doubt that ...
My own point of view is (that) ...

Emphasizing/smoothing opinions
absolutely
extremely
tremendously
enormously
exactly/about the same
gradually
partly
hardly

Expressing other people's opinions
According to ...
Those who think so argue that ...
Those who disagree claim that ...
Those who support this suggestion maintain that ...
They believe/say/claim (that) ...

Rejecting arguments
I'm not so sure that ...
I doubt that ...
This argument is simply nonsense.
It is foolish to believe that ...

Concluding
Summing up (we can say that) ...
All in all, ...
Taking everything into account, ...
In conclusion, ...
On the whole, ...